WHAT TITHING IS NOT

WHAT NATION IS HE SPEAKING TO?

Author

William Thomas Gregory

xulon

PRESS

infallible – Liable to be erroneous. Not capble of making a mistake

inerrantly – Not wrong

vitality – enduring quality, mental and physical vigor.

pinnacle – peak height of creation

pivtol – most or critical important

Loathsome – hate, dislike, greatly; Repulsive = disgust detest, rejection.

Sanction – To ratify, To Certify, to Approve, to Confirm, endorse

exegetical – explanation or critical interpretation
(exegesis)   of a text

deity – God   divinity – relating to, or being God. Superb supremely good, Heavenly. A divine Being (God)

propitiation – regain or gain the favor of

Typified – To represent by an image, form, model, or resemblance

propitiatory – regain or gain the favor of

dedicatory – to devote to the worship of a divine being to set Apart for a define purpose

Eucharistic – Communion

vicarious – change, alternation, stead; acting for another done or suffered by one person on behalf of another or others. Sharing in some one else's experience through the use of the imagination or sympathetic feelings.

Sanctified – Free From sin. Holiness. Set Apart

Consecrated – Set aside as sacred, to devote solemly to a purpose.

SECT – a Religious denomination

Vicarious = suffered by one person on behalf of another or others.

propitiation = to gain or regain the favor of buying off the purpose of Sin.

The mercy seat = the place which used for the the covering of the Ark. A place where the priest used to sprinkle the blood of the expiatory sacrifices on the great day of atonement, was where the Lord promised to meet His people. the word greek word for mercy seat is hilasterion Christ is designated as hilasterion Rm. 3:2

About The Author

I wrote this book in memory of my son, LaNier Robert Gregory; I am sorry he is not here. Sunrise: September 18, 1974 – Sunset: September 12, 1997, May God get all honor and glory. Glory and Honor belong to Him only, My Lord Jesus Christ. The truth has been in Darkness and secretly shut out of the light (make blind, deprive of mental or spiritual light, make spiritually blind, unable to see the truth about tithes,) My Son, rest in peace, see you when I get there, LOVE, POPS.

I am not writing this book to be honored by man or to be looked upon as though I did something great, I am writing this book for My Lord and God Jesus Christ. It's a pleasure to write this book for My Lord, because the truth has been hidden too long about what tithes are. So He will say to me "well done, my good and faithful servant." God always uses a person to do His will, I am well pleased that I can do this for Him, because God is not a man that He should lie about what tithes were or are. You cannot separate God from His word, God cannot contradict Himself, the word of God and the Spirit of God agree on all things concerning His word for He cannot be a true God and contradict Himself (to put scripture in the Bible saying tithes is money would be contradicting Himself, and He wouldn't be a true God.)

To you Pastors, knowing God's word about what tithes are, but not honoring or respecting His word about what tithes are not (Money), but who have turned to their own righteousness to lie in God's name for the Love of Money.

To God be the glory for His sustaining grace while this word was in the course of preparation. In all that I endeavored to write about I took it as a matter of course that a plain "thus said the Lord" is the final word on any subject under consideration about what tithes are not (MONEY). I have tried to convince the entire range of scriptures, on tithes (that limited space is what made you tell the truth on this subject.) I would like to have considered the subject at greater length, and the reader will no doubt find truths that will enrich the thoughts found in this book that might have been very materially improved and strengthened.

While the entire message is intended as an exposition of Christian doctrine on the truth about tithes, and offerings, my aim is to reach the hearts of Christians as well as their heads, to appeal to the conscience as well as to understanding of what tithes are, to make this message practical as well as exegetical. How well we succeeded or failed, by lying and saying that we should tithe, I will let you be your own judge Pastor, on your own righteousness or on your unrighteousness about tithes.

Another thing that should be mentioned is the whatever the point under discussion my aim was to quote just enough scripture to make the point clear and convincing, rather than to attempt to quote all scripture bearing on said point. I endeavored to make the message brief. The burden of this message is, upon our Lord's Holy Word, His infallible Word, to magnify the word of the Lord, and to endear the message of the Cross to the hearts of the readers, with a prayer that the blessing of the Lord may be added to the imperfect efforts put forth, and that the entire body of readers may be together in support of full truths of the Gospel, a "pure religion," and a united effort to make this Gospel known to all the world, I submit this message for your consideration, that Christ Jesus fulfilled the Law which required tithes and offerings in Hebrews 8:13, also in Romans 10:4 this is the end of that Law, we are now under a New Covenant, the Blood of Christ called the New Testament. Let us therefore hold fast to Christ. He and he alone, is our Hope and our Savior, for those who put their trust in Him.

Remember what Jesus said, God's Word is true. You should believe in God's word by faith. I believe if you turn from God's Word and believe what your Pastor says, and don't accept what His word says about tithes, then you have put your faith in your Pastor, and not in God's inspired Word. Abraham believed in God by faith, God says He is the truth, His Word is the only truth. Many Christians have let their Pastor take the truth of what His Word says, and they put their trust in their Pastor, when God has said, "I am the truth."

Remember when studying the Bible always find out how the message is used and what generation He is speaking to, then you will find out the truth on tithing. Acts 17:11, search the scripture daily as they did in Thessalonica. This truth has been hidden in darkness too long. Jesus said, "My word is true on tithes." (TITHES ARE NOT MONEY.)

Many Pastors are taking tithes. Jesus said, "You will know the tree by its fruit."

Many Pastors are teaching tithing, but God says in Romans 3:4, "May it never be." Rather, let God be found true, on what tithes are though every man be found a liar. As it is written, God is not a man that he should lie, and it is impossible to separate God from His word.

References Used

The Old Testament of the New Open Bible, study edition, New American Standard Bible.

Halley's Bible Handbook

Holy Bible, Old & New Testaments, People's Parallel Edition, King James Version, and The Living Bible.

Doctrines of the Bible.

Smith's Bible Dictionary.

The Lexicon Webster Dictionary.

Bible Dictionary.

Through the Bible in 55 Minutes

CONTENTS

Chapter 4   Pages 33 – 41

What God did to bring man back into fellowship with Him,
after Adam sinned and lost fellowship with Him, through sacrifice and offerings, God sectioned the nation of Israel. For example, the Levis, were called to the priesthood. They offered animal sacrifices for their sins, looking forward to the once-for all
infinite sacrifice of the Lamb of God. Animal offerings were
meant to be a picture of the perfect sacrifice of Christ on the Cross.

Chapter 5   Pages 43 - 45

Anything offered to God must be Holy.

Chapter 6   Pages 47 – 50

Focusing on the first man, giving offerings to God, Abel and Cain.

Chapter 7   Pages 51 – 66

God spoke in Malachi 3:8 about being robbed of offerings. Our
Churches are teaching that offerings are money, God is saying
He is being robbed. What were offerings used for? Offerings
have many meanings in today's society. An offering is generally understood to be a contribution of money to a Church.

Chapter 8   Pages 67 –102

These are scriptures used by the Seven-Day Adventist Church,
as some Baptist Churches, and the Church of God in Christ.
Many Churches use these scriptures in error, to misleading us into
believing their doctrine about tithes and offerings.

Chapter 1

What you should know about God's word. It is eternal, without error. His word is infallible, trustworthy, and not liable to errors on doctrine. God's word is eternal, so is God. His word is the same yesterday, today, and forever. Isaiah 40:8 says, "the grass withers, the flower fades, but the word of God stands forever.

The Bible is the greatest book ever written. In it God Himself is speaking to man. It is a book of divine instruction. It offers comfort in sorrow, guidance in perplexity, advice for our problems, rebuke for our sins, and daily inspiration for our need.

The Bible is not one simple book. It is an entire library of books covering the whole range of literature. It includes history, poetry, drama, biography, prophecy, philosophy, science and inspirational reading. Little wonder then that all or part of the Bible had been translated in more the 1,200 languages and every year more copies of the Bible are sold than any other single book.

The Bible alone truly answers the greatest questions that men of all ages have asked; where have I come from? Where am I going? Why am I here? How can I know the truth? For the Bible reveals the truth about God, explains the origin of man, points out the only way to salvation and eternal life, and explains the age-old problem of sin and suffering.

The great theme of the Bible is the Lord Jesus Christ and His work of redemption for mankind. The person and work of Jesus Christ is promised, prophesied and pictured in the types and symbols of the Old Testament. In all of His truth and beauty, the Lord Jesus Christ is revealed in all the Gospels. The full meaning of His Life, His death, and His resurrection are explained in the Epistles. His glorious coming again to earth in the future is unmistakably foretold in the Book of revelation. The great purpose of the written word of God, the Bible, is to reveal the living word of God, the Lord Jesus Christ. (Read John 1:1-18)

The Bible is not an end in itself, but rather a means to knowing God and doing His will. The Apostle Paul said, "be diligent to present yourself approved to God as a workman who does not need to be ashamed, handling accurately the word of Truth, (2 Timothy 2:15), God has given us the Bible in order that we might know Him and that we might do His will here on earth.

Devotional Bible study is the most important kind of Bible study. Devotional Bible study means reading and studying the word of God in order that we may hear God's voice, and that we may know how to do His will and to live a better Christian life.

The very best way to study the Bible is simply to read it daily, with close attention and with prayer, to see the light that shines from its pages, to meditate upon it, and to continue to reads it until somehow it works itself, its words, its expressions, its teachings, its habits of thought, and its presentation of God and His Christ – into the very warp and woof of one's being.

For your devotional reading and study of the Bible, here are several important, practical suggestions:

1. Begin your Bible reading with prayer. (Psalms 119:18) (John 16:13-15)

2. It is often very helpful, in looking for the true mean-

ing of a chapter or passage, to ask yourself the following questions.

- What is the main subject of this passage? ↰
- Who are the persons revealed in this passage? Who is God speaking to, about whom is He speaking, and what nation does He ask for tithes?

To meditate means to reflect, to ponder, and to consider, to dwell in thought. Through mediation, the word of God will become meaningful and real to you. The Holy Spirit will use this time to apply the word of God to your life and its problems. The second principle of interpretation is to interpret the Bible in light of its historical background.

Also interpret the Bible according to all of the parallel passages which deal with the subject, according to the message of the entire Bible.

The Bible reveals the nature of God as spirit, unity, and trinity. He is a spirit – a personal, infinite being (John 4:24). He is one – one in substance or nature and incapable of being divided into separate parts (Deuteronomy 6:4). He is three – eternally existing in three co-equal persons (Matthew 28:19). While great mystery surrounds God's nature, it is reassuring to know that our God is above us.

God's attributes are merely words we use to describe how God is and how He acts towards us. Among these attributes are love, holiness, constancy, justice, truth, eternality, omniscience (all knowing), omnipresence (everywhere present), and omnipotence (all powerful). The fact that we can grasp and understand this is much about God is evidence of God's desire that all people may know Him.

The word Father is variously applied in the Bible. When God is spoken of as the Father of all men, it is as Creator. As Father of Christ, it expresses an eternal, unique relationship. As the Father of believers, it denotes a relationship established by grace. As the Father of Israel, means a bond established by covenant. However

Father is used, it is a deliberately chosen word to communicate to men of the primary ways God wants us to conceive of Him. -

The title "Son of God" is one which Jesus never directly applied to Himself, but when others applied it to Him, Jesus willingly accepted it as a claim to His Own deity (John 10:24-38). Jesus often referred to Himself as "the Son" which was certainly an abbreviation for the Son of God. How significant is this term to the Christian? It is very important, because it helps establish some major truths without which we would be left with little evidence that the words of Jesus were actually true. It can be said that as our relationship with the Son of God determines whether we will become Christians, our relationship with the Spirit of God determines what kind of believers we will be.

Worship is essential also to spiritual growth. Worship involves honor and respect towards God, the ceremony of private and public worship, and joyful service of Christians to their Lord. Christians who submit to the Lordship of Christ in reverence and service will grow in their spiritual lives.

The Bible describes Christian life as walking by the Spirit (Galatians 5:6). Walking best represents the step-by-step character of the spiritual life. Living by the Spirit's power is a moment-by-moment yielding to the Spirit's will and control. The evidence that we are walking in the Spirit is simply the display of the Fruit of the Spirit (Galatians 5:22-23). Walking in the Spirit involves confession of sin, yielding to God, and being filled or controlled by the Spirit.

Mankind is by nature sinful and needs the righteousness of God. We must be separated from sin and set apart to righteousness. If we are to approach God, we must do so on God's terms. We must have new lives in which our sins have been forgiven and obliterated.

Also, always remember that the Bible is God's infallible, inerrantly inspired Word. There are no mistakes in the Bible. God

16

has included everything in the Bible that He wants you to know and is necessary for you to know concerning salvation and your Christian life.

Therefore, there is a need for Bible interpretation. This is a fascinating study in itself, but I want to give you just a few principles of interpretation of the Bible that will keep you from error and help you understand the difficult passages of the Word of God.

The second principle of interpretation is to interpret the Bible in the light of historical background. There are three aspects to this.

Study the personal circumstances of the writer. Studying the Bible is to understand the message of the entire scripture and its historical background, according to all the subjects, which God is speaking about, including to whom He is speaking to. Study the culture and customs of the country at the time that the writing or story was taking place.

 Every Bible book has its specific message and purpose intended by the Holy Spirit to bring some special message to man. Therefore, there is a need for Bible interpretation. Always interpret according to the correct meaning of words used. You can find the correct meaning of a word in several ways. Compare the usage of the word in other parts of the Bible to find how it was used in that generation. Another way is to look up its background or its root. You could do this with the use of a dictionary. Still another way is to look up the synonyms (words that are similar in meaning but slightly different), for example, prayer, intercession, supplication.

The Bible is not man speaking about God; it is about God's infallible word. We must realize the treasure it contains. God's word is infallible, exempt from error or moral failure, absolutely trustworthy.

Of all the possible sins against God, the most serious is that of self-will. This sin led to the fall of Satan (Is. 14:12-14), and can be said to be the root of Adam's transgression (Gen. 3:1-7). It is, therefore, of utmost importance that the child of God find His will and perform it.

The dismissal of doubt and strengthening of faith are best accomplished by reading and understanding the Word of God (Rom. 10:17). The Holy Spirit will convince the willing heart of its power. Growing in the Word produces growth in faith. Reading and understanding the Word is like planting seeds of faith in the heart. They will bear the mature fruit of faith. The mind that is occupied with the things of the Lord cannot at the same time be susceptible to temptation.

It is one thing to be convinced of the need for the new life, but it is an entirely different thing to acquire the new life. When we are "saved" we are said to be new creatures (2 Cor. 5:17), to pass from death to life (John 5:24); to transfer from the rule of darkness to the Kingdom of God's Son (Col. 1:13); to be born again (John 3:3); and be adopted by God (Gal. 4:4-5). These wonderful results of having new life in Christ are offered freely to all that trust in Christ for salvation.

One of the most thrilling benefits of finding new life in Christ is eternal (everlasting) life. We enter a new, personal relationship with God that gives us a fullness of spiritual vitality, and this new life is a gift that will never die. God can accomplish a life-changing transformation for all that truly believe in Christ. It can be said that our relationship with the Son of God determines whether we will become Christians, our relationship with the Spirit of God determines what kind of believers we will be. Knowing how to grow in the new life is essential. The old adage is ever true: sin will keep you from God's Word, and God's Word will keep you from sin.

Obey the Word of God. As Paul said to Timothy in Second Timothy 3:16, "All Scripture is inspired by God and is profitable for teaching, for reproof, for correction, for training in righteousness". The Bible has been given to us that we may live a holy life, well pleasing to God. Therefore God says, "prove yourselves doers of the word, and not merely hearers" (James 1: 22). Compare scripture with scripture to find its true meaning.

"All scripture is inspired by God," wrote the Christian Apostle Paul (1 Tim. 3:16). What does this mean? The phrase inspired of God the Greek word O-Ppneu-Stos literally means God breathed. A related Greek word, Pneu-Ma means spirithence, the claim is that God's Holy Spirit moved human writers, breathing on them, so that the end product could truthfully be called the Word of God, not that of man. Indeed, many who have studied the Bible marvel at its harmony, its scientific accuracy, the honesty and candor of its writers, and most important, its fulfilled prophecies, all of which have convinced millions of thinking readers that this book is from a source higher than man.

But how closely did God guide the writing of the Bible? Some say that He inspired merely the thoughts found in the Bible, not the words. Some say that He dictated the Bible verbatim. In reality, though, inspiration cannot be reduced to a single prophet, for God spoke in many ways to our forefathers by means of the prophets and the Holy Spirit (Heb. 1:1, compare 1st or 2nd Cor. 12-6.).

He that comes to God must first believe that He is divine, holy, and that He is Spirit, sinless, and that He is the same yesterday, today and forever. His word is true and cannot be changed. His word is the only truth. They that worship Him must worship Him in spirit and truth. As Christians we must honor and respect His word as the truth, and that cannot be change by any Pastor, or anyone else. In Hebrews 7:5, it says, "No one can take tithes but the Levis, who He called under the Law. In Hebrews 8:13, with new covenant, He has made the first obsolete. But whatever is being obsolete and growing old is ready to disappear. Tithes have never been money, says the Lord Jesus Christ. It is the truth and without error. Isaiah 40:8 says, "The grass withers, the flower fades, but the Word of God stands forever." God said, in Matthew 24:35, that tithes were never money. "Heaven and earth shall pass away, but My words shall not pass away." My Holy Scripture stands forever. As Christians and Pastors we must believe that his word is infallible. His word is spiritual. Sin will keep you from His word and His word will keep you from sin.

The Bible instructs us in what we are to do.

The Bible provides us with a sword for victory over sin.

The Bible makes our lives fruitful.

The Bible gives power to our prayers.

The Bible strengthens us.

Chapter 2

Our Christian Pastors have forgotten the righteousness of God's word, and what His Holy Word says about tithes and offerings. The only scripture that offerings were money is Exodus 25:1-3. These offerings were for building the Tabernacle.

Millions of Christians are paying tithes in their church today. When asked why they pay tithes, all explain that this is what their Church teaches for us to pay tithes. They have not searched the scripture (Acts 17:11) to find out if this is the truth or not. Most say that their Church's Pastor teaches them if they don't pay tithes and offerings, God says in Malachi 3:8 we are robbing Him. Our Church's Pastors all say this is our offering to God, and that this is Scriptural. I will search the scriptures to find out if it is true or false. Because most Christians listen to whatever their Pastor says about tithes, and they believe that their Pastors are teaching Scriptural truth. They receive it with open minds, cherishing it for one purpose, thinking it must be God's will, never questioning what their Pastor said about tithes. They never study to see if it is true or not. They believe that their Pastors would not teach them error or mislead them just for the love of money.

ⵏ   If Christians would only begin to do as Paul said in 2nd
Timothy 2:15, they would surely learn and know what is true.
"Study to show thyself approved unto God, a workman that
need not be ashamed, rightly dividing the word of truth."

Christians should respect their Pastor's teachings, but
remember what the Apostle Paul said. As Christians we should
not continue to abandon these principles, but accept their different purpose. "Now these were more noble minded than those in
Thesalonica, for they received the word with great eagerness,
examining the scriptures daily to see wheter these things were so.ⵏ

Paul is saying in 2nd Timothy 2:15, to study that we
Christians can know the truth, so no one can deceive us through
philosophy or doctrine. God has no beginning. His word is ever-
lasting, continuing without interruption. Perpetual means continuing or continued without intermission or interruption.
Hebrews 8:13 says the law is ended which concerned tithes. Paul
is saying if Christians study the scriptures, they will find out in
Hebrews chapter 8 that Christ brought to mankind a New
Covenant. The first Covenant, which centered on the Tabernacle
Service and the Ten Commandments, has served its purpose. The
first Covenant was Temporal, Christ's Covenant would be
Everlasting (13:20). The First Covenant was sealed with the blood
of animals. Christ's Covenant was sealed with His Own Blood
(10:29). It was a better Covenant with better promises, based on
the Immutability of God's Word (6:18). The High Priest offered
the blood of animals, Christ offered His Own Blood (9:12).
Once for all (26:28) Christ offered Himself. The New Covenant
is here called "The New Testament". A Testament is a will, a
bequest to heirs, effective only after the death of the maker.
The New Covenant is the Will, which Christ made for His heirs,
which could not become effective until, by His death, He had
atoned for their sins.

Most major churches are teaching that tithes apply to us today. They use these scriptures, (Leviticus 27:30-32) (Malachi 3:8-10) (Matthew 23:23), to suggest that God is saying this is scriptural for us today. I have searched and studied the Holy Scriptures to rightly divide the Word of Truth about tithes for three years and six months so now I will let you know the truth about tithes not being money. This practice of unrighteousness by Pastors God called to shepherd His flock of His Church faithful to His word, not for the love of money, but willingly, not filthy lucre, but of a ready mind.

Is our church transgressing the Word of God by turning away from the truth about tithing? Have church Pastors forgotten the righteousness of God's inspired word, that His word is infallible? Is our church Pastors, who shepherd God's flock, receiving on doctrine, or a tradition of man's, about tithes? Have our Pastors forgotten God's word is without error and is eternal?

When I asked my Pastor, Rev. Chris Le Grande about tithing, I said that God called only the Levi. is to take tithes. "And verily they are the sons of Jacob" received the office of the priesthood. They had a commandment to take tithes of the people according to the Law. I said the Bible said their brethren were of the Twelve Tribes of Israel. This is whom God told them to take tithes from. So I said to my Pastor that only God can call a person to the office of priesthood, and only God can give this commandment to take tithes, and He gave this commandment to the Levis. At the time, we were without Christ, being excluded from the commonwealth of Israel and strangers from the Covenants of Promise, having no hope and without God in the world. I will let you see from God's Holy Scriptures, what tithes were and where the tenth came from.

My Pastor said that we became Levis, through Abraham, this is why he takes tithes. I told him to read Galatians 3:26, which says, "For you are all sons of God through faith in Christ

23

Jesus." If you belong to Christ, then you are Abraham's off-springs, heirs, according to the promise. I said, "You are not a Levite; Levites are Abraham's descendants; and we are not his descendants. We are Gentiles." Galatians 13:28 says, "There is neither Jew or Greek, there is neither slave nor free man, there is neither male nor female, for you are all one in Christ Jesus." I said to my Pastor, "I don't see how you can become a Levite, by being in Abraham's seed, the Bible doesn't say anything like that; we are all sons of God through Christ Jesus (Gal. 3:26) (Rom. 8:14). For all who are being led by the Spirit of God, these are the sons of God. ↑

How can you, Bishop Clarence McZendon, say on tele-vision, that if members of your congregation don't pay tithes, then they don't have a seat in your church? Christ died for His church, not you. To ask for tithes is false and unrighteous, mis-leading and deceitful; you're lying about God's word. (Read 1st Pet. 5:2; 2:25; 5:2) The duties of the Bishop and elders appear to have been as follows – general superintendence over the spir-itual well being of the flock. 1st Peter 5:2 says, "Feed the flock of God, which is among you, taking the oversight thereof; not by constraint, but willingly; not for filthy lucre, but of a ready mind." Tithes are not money, Bishop Clarence McZendon, what you are teaching about tithes is false. You are doing this for one thing, which is for the love of money. Tithes were for the Nation of Israel only, (read Heb. 7:5) who God called to take tithes. (Isaiah 40:8) Read this scripture. (1st Thess. 5:12; Titus 1:9; 1st Tim. 5:17)

My Pastor should have read Galatians 3:14. You don't become a Levite through Abraham. In Christ Jesus, the bless-ing of Abraham will come to the Gentiles, so that we might receive the promise of spirit through faith. My Pastor should have read Galatians 3:7-9. It is those who are of faith who are sons of Abraham. The scriptures foresaw that God would justify the

Gentiles by faith.

Are our churches Pastors teaching a scheme, a trick for advantage or for gain? Tithes are not for us and have never been for us, and tithes are not money. I will show you from God's Holy Scriptures what tithes were and whom He called to take tithes and what tithes were used for. Our church Pastors are teaching a tradition, handed down as doctrine, which is really just a mistaken belief. God said to preach the truth about His Word on tithes. Pastors have an obligation to teach the truth about His infallible word.

Later on in this book I will show you what God's word says about what tithes were and what they were used for.

Chapter Three

Focusing on Adam and the Creation, Adam losing fellowship with God.

Ref. The New Open Bible, New American Standard Genesis, page 1-2. The first part of Genesis focuses on the beginning of sin in the world and culminate in the devastating flood in the days of Noah. The second part of the book focuses on God's dealings with one man, Abraham, through whom God promises to bring salvation and blessings to the world. Abraham and his descendants learn firsthand that it is always safe to trust in the Lord in times of famine and feasting, blessings and bondage. From Abraham, to Isaac, to Jacob, to Joseph, God's promises begin to come to fruition in a great nation possessing a great land.

Christ is also seen in people and events that serve as type. (A "type" is a historical fact that illustrates a spiritual truth.) Adam is a type of "Him who is to come" (Rom. 5:14). Both entered the world, through a special act of God, as sinless men. Adam is the head of the old creation. Christ is the head of the new creation. Abel's acceptable offering of blood sacrifice points to Christ, and there is a parallel in his murder of Cain. Melchizedek (righteous king) is "made like the Son of God" (Heb. 7:3). He is King of Salem (peace) who brings forth bread and wine and is the priest of the Most High God. Joseph is also a type of Christ. Joseph and Christ are both objects of special love by their fathers. Both are hated by their brothers; both are rejected as rulers over their brothers; both are conspired against and sold for silver; both are condemned though innocent; and both are raised from humiliation to glory by the power of God.

Genesis gives the beginning of almost everything, including the beginning of the universe, life, man, Sabbath, death, marriage, sin, redemption, family, literature, cities, art, language and sacrifices and offerings.

"And I will put enmity between you and the woman, and between your seed and her seed; He will bruise you on the head, and you shall bruise Him on the heel."

"And I will bless those who bless you, and the one who curses you I will curse. And in you all families of the earth shall be blessed."

Genesis, Chapter 15, central to all of scripture is the Abrahamic Covenant which is given in Genesis 12:1-3 and ratified in 15:1-21. Israel receive three specific promises:

1. The promise of a great land, "from the rivers of Egypt as far as the great river, the Euphrates" (Gen. 15:18)
2. The promise of a great nation, "And I will make your descendants as the dust of the earth." (Gen. 13:16)
3. The promise of a great blessing, "And I will bless you, and make your name great; and so you shall be a blessing." (Gen. 12:2)

Genesis is not so much a history of man as it is the first chapter in the history of the Redemption of Man. As such, Genesis is a highly selective spiritual interpretation of history. Genesis is divided into four great events (1-11) and four great people (12-50).

Chapters 1-11 lay the foundation upon which the entire Bible is built and centers on four key events.

  1. Creation: God is the sovereign Creator of matter, energy, space, and time. Man is the pinnacle of the Creation. ✓
  2. The Fall: is followed by corruption. In the first sin man is separated from God.
  3. Adam from God: in the second sin, man is separated from man (Cain and Abel.
  4. Inspite of the devastating curse that followed sin, God promises hope of redemption through the seed of a woman (3:15) (3).

As man multiplies, sin also multiplies, until God is compelled to destroy humanity, with the exception of Noah and his family. Genesis teaches the unity of the human race; we are all children of Adam through Noah, but because of rebellion at the Tower of Babel, God fragments the single culture and language of the post-flood world and scatter people over the face of the earth.

Once the nation were scattered, God focuses on one man and his descendants through whom He will bless all nations (Gen. 12:50)

  1. Abraham: The calling of Abraham (Gen. 12) is the pivotal point of the book. The three covenant promises God made to Abraham; land descendants and blessings are foundational to his program of bringing salvation to the earth.
  2. Isaac: God establishes His covenant with Isaac as the spiritual link with Abraham.
  3. Jacob: God transforms this man from selfishness to servanthood and changes his name to Israel, the

father of the Twelve Tribes of Israel.

 4. Joseph: Jacob's favorite son suffers at the hands of his brothers and become a slave in Egypt. After his dramatic rise to the ruler of Egypt, Joseph delivers his family from famine and brings them out of Canaan to Goshen.

Genesis ends on a note of impending bondage with the death of Joseph. There is great need for the redemption that was to follow in the Book of Exodus.

Adam lost fellowship with God.

The original sin does not seem to be a very great sin, from man's perspective. All he did was take a bite of some fruit; Adam's sin is serious because the fruit was of the Tree of Knowledge, of good and evil, of which God said that he (Adam) was not to eat under penalty of death. Up to this time Adam was morally innocent. When he sinned, he became a sinner by nature. He died spiritually. After sinning, he lost fellowship with God. After the fall of Adam, Adam and all mankind lost fellowship with God. So God drove the man Adam out, therefore the Lord God sent him out from the garden. Not only Adam, but also, the serpent was cursed, and all cattle and every beast of the field were cursed. The serpent, used by Satan to affect the fall of man, is cursed. The curse effected, the instrument, the serpent, but also the indwelling energizer, Satan. Great physical changes took place in the serpent. It was upright, now it must go on its belly. It was the most desirable animal of the animal creation, now it is the most loathsome. The sight or thought of a snake should evoke the devastating effects of sin.

Adam became a sinner before Eve conceived a child. Thus, every human being descended from him, is a sinner, just like him, except Christ Jesus. Because of Adam's sin, death entered into the human race. Every human being needs to have the new life. Adam was the first man to live upon the face of the earth. From Adam and Eve came every other human being who ever lived upon the face of the earth. Thus Adam is the head, from whom every other man came. Like begets like. Apples beget apples, dogs beget dogs, and human beings beget human beings.

Chapter 4

W hat God did to bring man back in fellowship with Him, after Adam sinned. God selected the nation of Israel. The Levites were called to the priesthood. They offered animal sacrifices for their sins, looking forward to the once-for all infinite sacrifice of the Lamb of God. Animal offerings were meant to be a picture of the perfect sacrifice of Jesus Christ on the Cross.

Ref. Smith Bible Dic.; page 577. Scripture represents God Himself as approaching man to point out and sanction the way by which the broken covenants should be restored.

Ref. Lex. Web. Dic.; page 849. Sanction, means that God made sacred, to ratify, confirm, as to sanction a law or covenant. His covenant was an agreement between two or more persons to do or refrain from doing some act. This convenant was made by God with the Nation of Israel.

God set forth, by putting forward to offer for consideration, a system of offering, and sacrifice, tithes; God said in Num. 18:26, "Moreover, you shall speak to the Levites and say to them, when you take from the sons of Israel the tithe which I have given you from them for your inheritance, then you shall present an offering from it to the Lord, a tenth of the tithes." A tenth of it an offering is a sacrifice. Ref, Lex. Web. Dic., page 844; says a sacrifice, the offering of an animal or possession to a deity, in propitiation means an atoning sacrifice or anything which propitiate, which Adam fell and was separated from Him. The scripture shows offerings and sacrifice to be a scheme proceeding from God and His foreknowledge. Sacrifice and offering was the method God chose to make satisfaction for their sins. Sacrificing was a ritual through which the Hebrew people offered the blood or flesh of an animal to God in payment for their sins.

Ref. Smith.Bible.Dic., page 577. This is what God did in His foreknowledge, the sacrifice system was fixed in all its parts until He (Christ) should come, whom sacrifice typified.

Ref. New Open Bible, New American Standard, page 1418 says, scripture shows that offerings and sacrifice was the method God chose for them to make satisfaction for their sins. In the Old Testament, animal sacrifice and offering were looking forward for all infinite sacrifice of the Lamb of God. God was satisfied with the true sacrifice, offering of His Son.

Christ stands out alone as the mediator between God and man, and His sacrifice is offered once and for all never to be imitated or repeated. It is an essential characteristic that He stands absolutely alone, offering His sacrifice without reference to faith or the conversion. With these views of our Lord's sacrifice on earth, as typified in the book of Leviticus, sacrifice on the altar. As without the sins offering of the cross this, our burnt offerings would be impossible. Our Lord is declared to have been fore-ordained (1 Peter 1:20) as a sacrifice before the foundation of the World. Sacrifice represented this great atonement as already made and accepted in God's foreknowledge, and to those who grasped the ideas of sin, pardon and self-dedication symbolized in them, they were the means of entering in the blessing which the one true sacrifice alone prepared.

Ref.Lex.Web.Dic., page 587. The material sacrifice, the substance or substance to a (Deity) God for some religious purpose. This is what God is saying, He's being robbed of.

Ref.Bible Dic., Page 169. Offering embraced the burnt sin, trespass, peace, and meat offering. These offerings, and sacrifices, pointed forward to Christ, the true sacrifice for sins. They were the shadow cast backward through the centuries by the Cross, the shadow of things to come which the Apostle Paul spoke of in Col. 2:17, "Things which are a mere shadow of what is to come, but the substance belongs to Christ". (Body of Christ) (Heb 8:5) ("That serve a copy and shadow of the heavenly things, just as Moses was warned by God, when he was about to erect the tabernacle." For see He says, that you make all things According to the pattern, which was shown you on the mountain. Heb. 10:1, "For the Law, since it has only a shadow of the good things to come and not the very from of things, can never by the same sacrifices year by year, which they offer continually, make perfect those who draw near."

These offerings of material substances were things, which are a mere shadow of what is to come, but the substance belongs to Christ. Shadow is the root, a figure projected in silhouette on the ground or other surface by means of interception of light.

✳ This is why God started a system of offering, tithes, and sacrifices. God foreordained a system of offering, tithe, and sacrifice before the World began, knowing that Adam would sin and loose fellowship with Him, so God's system of tithes, offerings, and sacrifices was fixed in all parts to bring mankind back into fellowship with Him. Adam was separated from God, died spiritually.

✳ These sacrifices and offerings for sin is the method, God chose to make satisfaction for sin, Ref. New Open Bible, New American Standard, page 1418.

Ref. Smith Bible Dic., page578. From the prophets and

35

the Epistles to the Hebrews we learn that the sin offering represents that covenant as broken by man and as knit together again
by God's appointed time, through the shedding of blood. The
shedding of blood, the symbol of life, signified that the death of
the offender was deserved for sin, but that the death of the victim was accepted for his death by the ordinance of God's mercy.
God's ordinance means a law, edict, or decree established by
authority; an established rite or ceremony, a decree of God or fate.
Beyond all doubt the sin offering distinctly witnessed that sin
existed in man, that the wages of sin were death, "and the God
had provided an atonement by the vicarious suffering of an
appointed victim. The ceremonial and meaning of the burnt offerings were very different. The idea of expiation seems not to have
been absent from it, for the blood was sprinkled round about the
altar of sacrifice, but the main idea is the offering of the whole
victim to God, representing as the laying of the hand on its head
shows the devotion of the sacrifice, body and soul, to Him.
Romans 12:1. the death of the victim was, so to speak, an inci-
dental feature. The meat offerings, the peace or thanks offerings,
the first fruits, etc., were simply offerings to God of His own best
gifts, as a sign of thankful homage, and as a means of maintaining
His service and His servants. The characteristic ceremony in the
peace offering was the eating of the flesh by the sacrificer. It beto-
kened the enjoyment of communion with God. It is clear from
this that the idea of sacrifice is a complex idea, involving the propitiatory, the dedicatory and the Eucharistic elements. Any one
of these, taken by itself, would lead to error and superstition. All
three probably were more or less implied in each sacrifice, each
element predominating in its turn. The Epistles to the Hebrews
contains the key of the whole sacrifice doctrine. The objects of
the Epistles are to show the typical and probationary character
of sacrifices, and to assert that in virtue of it alone they had spiritual meaning. Our Lord is declared (see 1 Pet. 1:20) to have been

foreordained; as a sacrifice before the foundation of the world, or, as it is more strikingly expressed in Revelations 13:8, "slain from the foundation of the World." "The material substance sacrificed was animal, and represented this great atonement as already made and accepted in God's foreknowledge; and those who grasped the ideas of sin, pardon and self-dedication symbolized in them, they were the means of entering into the blessings which the one true sacrifice alone procured. They could convey nothing in themselves; yet as "types" they might, if accepted by a true though necessarily imperfect faith, by means of conveying in some degree the blessings of the anti-type. It is clear that the atonement, the Epistles to the Hebrews, as in the New Testament generally, is viewed in a twofold light. On the one hand it is set forth distinctly as a vicarious sacrifice, means performed or suffered for, or instead of another; filling the place of another; serving as a substitute or deputy, as Christ did when He became our substitute on the Cross, which was rendered necessary by the sins of man, and in which the Lord "bore the sins of many." It is essential characteristic that in it He stands out alone as the mediator between God and man; and His sacrifice is offered once for all, never to be imitate or repeated. Now, this view of atonement is set forth in the Epistles as typified by the sin offering. On the other hand the sacrifice of Christ is set forth to us as the completion of that perfect obedience to the will of the Father which is the natural duty of sinless man. The main idea of this view of the atonement is representative rather than vicarious. It is typified by the burnt offering. As without the sin offering of the Cross, our burnt offering would to us be unavailing. With these views of our Lord's sacrifice on earth, as typified in the Levitical sacrifices on the outer altar, is also to be connected with the offering of His intercession for us in Heaven, which was represented by the incense. The typical sense of the meat offering or peace offering is less connected with the sac-

37

rifice of Christ Himself than with those sacrifices of praise, thanksgiving, charity and devotion which we, as Christians, offer to God, and "with which He is well pleased", (Heb. 13:15-16), "as with an odor of sweet smell, a sacrifice acceptable to God," (Phillip. 4:18).

This is what God used tithes for as a sacrifice, offering, offered to Him as a sin sacrifice for the sins of the Nation of Israel, to bring them back in fellowship with Him. These sacrifices pointed to Christ and typified Him. He foreordained that tithes were to be used as sacrifices through which the Hebrew people offered the blood and flesh of animals to God in payment for their sins. Without the shedding of blood, there is no remission for sin.

Our church Pastors are teaching God's inspired word falsely, by teaching tithes are a tenth of your money, and that tithes are money. They teach that God is saying in Malachi 3:8 that He is being robbed out of money. Here is what offerings were used for.

Now you will read from God's Holy inspired Word. God never said anything about offerings being money. The sacrifice system was in place long before the law came in. Ref. The New Open Bible, New American Standard-page-119-1426. (Gen. 4:4) Abel offered the firstlings of his flock as a sacrifice. Read (Lev. 27:26). In this scripture God foreordained, before the foundation of the World, that all first-born animals belonged to Him. In Num. 3:13 "All the first-born are Mine, on the day that I struck down all the first-born in the land of Egypt, I sanctified to Myself all the first-born in Israel. From man to beast. They shall be Mine; I am the Lord." Ex. 13-2, Deu. 15-19 - God foreordained, before the foundation of the World, that the firstling of Abel's flock are His. "I sanctified them to Myself." The burnt offering involved a male animal wholly consumed by fire on the altar. The burnt offering typified Christ's total offering in submission to His Father's will. These offerings came out of tithes.

38

These were God's Statutes and Ordinances, His Commandments, Law, and Covenant. Num. 18:26 "Moreover, you shall speak to the Levites and say to them, When you take from the sons of Israel the tithe which I have given you from them for your inheritance, then you shall present an offering from it to the Lord, a tenth of the tithe, a tenth part of the tithe. God is saying, in Num. 18:26, out of your tithe, to present to Him a tenth part as a offering, offered to Him for sin, to bring the nation of Israel in fellowship with Him. After Adam sinned, and was separated from Him, he died spiritually (2Chron 31:6) "And the sons of Israel and Judah who lived in the cities of Judah also brought in the tithe of oxen and sheep, and the tithe of sacred gifts which were consecrated to the Lord their God." (Deu.14:23) "The tithe of your grain, your new wine, your oil, and the first-born of your herd and flock." There are more scriptures on tithes, in Deu.14-Num.18-Neh.10-13 chapter.

The Law of the Tithes

Deu.14:22-23 "You shall surely tithe all the produce from what you sow, which comes out of the field every year. (28) At the end of every third year you shall bring out all the tithe of your produce in that year, and shall deposit it in your town."

Now you will read from God's Holy infallible Word that anything offered to God must be Holy, sanctified and consecrated. Don't you know, Pastor, God can not accept money because He is Holy, anything offered to Him must be pure and undefiled. Offerings and tithes are not money. This is why God sanctified us.

The burnt offering typifies Christ's total offering in submission to His Father's Will. The meal offering typifies Christ's sinless service. Lev. 2:1 "Now when anyone presents a grain

39

offering as an offering to the Lord, his offering shall be of fine flour, and he shall pour oil on it and put frankincense on it." More in Lev. 2:1-16. The meal offering, or grain offering, describe in Leviticus (2) was similar in purpose to the burnt offering. The grain was brought to the priest who threw a portion on the fire, accompanied by the burning of incense.

The peace offering typifies the fellowship believers have with God through the word of the cross. Lev. 3:1 "Now if his offering is a sacrifice of peace offerings, if he is going to offer out of the herd, whether male or female, he shall offer it without defect before the Lord."

The peace offering was a ritual meal shared with God, the priests, and often other worshippers. (Lev.3) A voluntary animal offering expressed praise to God and fellowship with others.

The sin offering typifies Christ as our guilt-bearer. Lev. 4:1 (1) "Then the Lord spoke to Moses, saying, (2) Speak to the sons of Israel, saying, If a person sins unintentionally in any of the things which the Lord has commanded not to be done, and commits them (3) If the anointed priest sins so to bring guilt on the people, then let him offer to the Lord a bull without defect as a sin offering for the sin he has committed."

The sin offering, also known as the guilt offering, was offered to make atonement for sins for which restitution was not possible (Lev. 4:5-12).

The trespass offering typifies Christ's payment for the damage of sin.

The guilt offering, Lev. 5:14 "Then the Lord spoke to Moses, saying, (15) If a person acts unfaithfully and sins unintentionally against the Lord's holy things, then he shall bring his guilt offering to the Lord: a ram without defect from the flock, according to the valuation in silver by shekels, in terms of the shekel of the sanctuary, for a guilt offering. (16) The priest shall then make atonement for him with the ram of the guilt offering, and it shall be forgiven him."

The guilt offering was made for lesser or unintentional offenses for which restitution was possible (Lev. 5:14-19).

Chapter 5

(Anything offered to God must be holy.)

God is saying in Lev. 7:1 that "His offering must be holy. Now this is the law of the guilt offering; it is most holy."

God is saying in Lev. 6:17 that "His offering must be holy. It shall not be baked with leaven. I have given it as their share from My offerings by fire; it is most holy, like the sin offering and the guilt offering."

God is saying in Lev. 6:25 that "His offering must be holy. He spoke to Aaron and to his sons, saying, This is the law of the sin offering; in the place where the burnt offering is slain the sin offering shall be slain before the Lord; it is most holy."

God is saying in Lev. 27:9 that His offering must be holy. Now if it is an animal of the kind which men can present as an offering to the Lord, any such that one gives to the Lord shall be holy.

God is saying in Lev. 27:10 "He shall not replace it or exchange it, a good for a bad, or a bad for good; or if he does exchange animal for animal, then both it and its substitute shall become holy."

God is saying in Lev. 27:26 that His offering must be holy. However, a first-born among animals, which as a first-born belongs to the Lord, no man may consecrate it, whether ox or sheep, it is the Lord's. Ex. 13:2

God is saying in Lev. 27:30 that His offering must be holy. Thus all the tithes of the land, of the seed of the land, or of the fruit of the tree, is the Lord's; it is holy to the Lord.

God is saying in Lev. 27:32 His offering must be holy. And for every tenth part of the herd or flock, whatever passes under the rod, the tenth one shall be holy to the Lord.

Lev. 26:46 "These are the statute and ordinances and laws which the Lord established between Himself and the sons of Israel through Moses at Mount Sinai."

Lev. 27:34 "These are the commandments which the Lord commanded Moses for the sons of Israel at Mount Sinai."

Lev. 7:37 "This is the law of the burnt offering, the grain offering, the sin offering, the guilt offering, the ordination offering, and the sacrifice or peace offering."

Lev. 7:38 "Which the Lord commanded Moses at Mount Sinai in the day that He commanded the sons of Israel to present their offerings to the Lord in the wilderness of Sinai."

God is holy, free from guilt or the defilement of sin. He is pure. His holiness is associated with His divinity. The Israelites serve a holy God, which requires them to be holy as well. To be holy is to be set apart or separated. They are to be separated from other nations unto God. God must be approached by the sacrificial offering, by the mediation of the priest, by purification of the nation from uncleanness, and by the provision for national cleansing and fellowship to worship a holy God. Lev. 19:1-2 "Then the Lord spoke to Moses, saying, speak to all the congregation of the sons of Israel and say to them, You shall be holy, for the Lord your God am holy."

God is holy, anything offered to Him must be holy, sacred, and sanctified. Money is defiled and not holy, unfit as a sacrifice to God.

God is saying to Moses in Ex. 28-Lev. 8:9 to consecrate

his brother Aaron and his sons. The priesthood was set within the tribe of Levi. Num. 3:44-45 "Then the Lord spoke to Moses, saying (45) Take the Levites instead of all the first-born among the sons of Israel and the cattle of the Levites. And, the Levites shall be Mine; I am the Lord." When God accepts anything, He always sanctifies and consecrates it and makes it holy, because of His Holiness. He had to make the Levites holy and cattle holy because He is holy and pure. This is why He said the tenth animal out of the herd or flock offered to Him must be holy. He never said in His holy scripture that tithes were money

Aaron and his sons were Levites. God said in Num. 3:12 "Now, behold, I have taken the Levites from among the sons of Israel instead of every first-born. The first issue of the womb among the sons of Israel, so the Levites shall be Mine." Anything or person God says is His, He sanctified because He is holy and cannot accept things or persons that are unclean or unfit. They must be free from extraneous elements. They must be free from guilt or the defilement of sin. Money is not.

2 Tim. 1:9 says "God called us, with a holy calling." Deu. 7:6 "For you are a holy people to the Lord your God." Rom. 12:1 "To present your bodies a living and holy sacrifice, acceptable to God which is your spiritual service of worship." Eph. 1:4 "That we should be holy and blameless before Him.".

There are more scriptures in the Bible on God only accepting holy things, and we shall be holy as He is holy. When we come to God, He sanctifies us to set up apart for holy or religious uses.

Chapter 6

Focusing on the first man, giving offerings to God — Abel and Cain. Gen. 4:4 "And, Abel, on his part, also brought of the firstlings of his flock and of their fat portions and the Lord had regard for Abel and his offering."

Ref. King James Version, page 11, back of Bible - The firstlings Abel brought of his flock represented the eldest; the earliest fruits harvested. The consecration of the first of the male children, of animals, and of fruits was an important part of the religion of Israel.

The Lord smote all the first-born in Egypt from man to beast, Ex. 12:29 "Now it came about at midnight that the Lord struck all the first-born in the land of Egypt, from the first-born of Pharaoh who sat on his throne to the first-born of the captive who was in the dungeon, and all the first-born cattle."

God said in Num. 3:13 "For all the first-born are Mine, on the day that I struck down all the first-born in the land of Egypt, I sanctified to Myself all the first-born in Israel, from man to beast. They shall be Mine. I am the Lord."

Abel's acceptable offering of blood sacrifice points to Christ, the true sacrifice, slain before the foundation of the World. Ref. The New Open Bible New American Standard.

Ref. Smith Bible Dic, page 194 - The law ordered in general that the first of all ripe fruits and of liquors, or as it is twice expressed, the first of fruits, should be offered in God's house Ex. 22:29 — It was an act of allegiance to God as the giver of all, no exact quantity was commanded.

Ref. New Open bible New American Standard, page 115 - the first fruits speak of Christ's resurrection, as the first-fruit of the resurrection of all believers. (1 Cor. 15:20-21-23.) Christ rose on the day of the first Fruits. (20) But now Christ has been raised from the dead, the first fruits of those who are asleep. (21) For since by a man came death, by a man also came the resurrection of the dead. (22) For as in Adam all die, so also in Christ all shall be made alive. (23) But each in his own order; Christ the first-fruits, after that those who are Christ's at His coming.

Christ rose on the day of the first fruits. Pentecost speaks of the descent of the Holy Spirit after Christ's ascension.

Heb. 11:4 By faith Abel offered to God a better sacrifice offering than Cain, through which he obtained the testimony that he was righteous, God testifying about His gifts.

God did not have regard for Cain's offering, because it was only fruits of the ground. Abel's offering was accepted because it was from the firstling of his flock and the fat portion. God accepted Abel's offering because it represented an allegiance to God as the giver of all. The firstlings represented Christ as the first resurrection of all believers.

Scripture shows, long before the Law, Abel made offering to God of the firstlings of his flock, and their fat portion. Later on, Noah built an altar and offered every clean animal and every clean bird, and offered burnt offerings on the altar. Noah offered to God a sacrifice of thanksgiving after the flood. Ref. New Open Bible New American Standard, page 119 - Most of these sacrifices involved the shedding of blood, a method God instituted to prepare His people for the Messiah's ultimate sacrifice for sins.

Represent

The burnt offering involved a male animal, animal wholly consumed by fire. The animal was killed and the priest collected the
blood and sprinkled it about the altar. The burning symbolized
the worshipper's desire to be purged of sinful acts. The burnt
offering typified Christ's total offering in submission to His
Father's will.

Gen. 22:2 "And He said, Take now your son, your only
son, whom you love, Isaac, and go to the land of Moriah; and offer
him there as a burnt offering on the mountains of which I will
tell you."

Gen. 22:13 "Then Abraham raised his eyes and looked,
and behold, behind him a ram caught in the thicket by his horns;
and Abraham went and took the ram, and offered him up for a
burnt offering in the place of his son." The burnt offering
Abraham offered to God represented the same kind of offering
Noah offered to God.

Ex. 8:25 "And Pharaoh called for Moses and Aaron
and said, Go, sacrifice to your God within the land."

Ex. 10:24 "Then Pharaoh called it to Moses, and said Go,
serve the Lord; only let your flocks and your herd be detained.
Even your little ones may go with you."

Ex. 10:25 "But Moses said, You must let us have sacrifice and burnt offerings, that we may sacrifice them to the Lord
our God."

Ex. 10:26 "Therefore, our livestock, too, will go with us;
not a hoof will be left behind, for we shall take some of them to
serve the Lord our God, and until we arrive there, we ourselves
do not know with what we shall serve the Lord."

Ex. 18:12 "Then Jethro, Moses' father-in-law, took a
burnt offering and sacrificed for God, and Aaron came with all
the elders of Israel to eat a meal with Moses' father-in-law
before God."

Ex. 20:24 "God said you shall make an altar of earth for Me, and you shall sacrifice on it your burnt offerings and your offerings, your sheep and your oxen in every place where I cause My name to be remembered, I will come to you and bless you."

New Open Bible New American Standard, page 88 The Mosaic Covenant was added alongside the Abrahamic Covenant so that the people of Israel would know how to conduct their lives until the Seed, the Christ, came to make the complete and perfect sacrifice, which the sacrifice of the Mosaic covenant only points to. The Mosaic covenant was never given so that by keeping it, people could be saved, but so that they might realize that they cannot do what God wants them to do, even when God writes it down on tablets of stone. The Law was given that man might realize that he is helpless and hopeless when left to himself and realize that his only hope is to receive the righteousness of God by faith in Jesus Christ.

Now that you have seen that God is Omniscient, All-Knowing, Knowing before the foundation of the World that these offerings of Abel, Noah, and Abraham would later become tithes. Num. 18:26. 2Chor:31-6

These offerings were the method God chose for the nation of Israel to offer for their sins, after Adam sinned and lost fellowship with Him. In the Old Testament, animal sacrifices were pictures looking forward to the once-for all infinite sacrifice of the Lamb of God. Ref. New Open Bible New American Standard, page 1418.

Chapter 7

When God said in Malachi 3:8 about being robbed of offerings, churches are teaching offerings are money. Our church Pastors are teaching that we are robbing God of money if we don't pay tithes and offerings, as He said in Malachi 3:8.

The Bible is God's infallible word, exempt from liability to error. There are no mistakes in God's word, it is eternal. Deu. 11:1 "On God's ordinance, You shall therefore love the Lord your God, and always keep His charge, His statutes, His ordinance and His commandments."

Num. 15:40 God's ordinances and statutes were His Laws, given to Moses, in order that they may remember to do all His commandments and be holy to their God. Lev. 2:6-15 was God's covenant and His ordinances and statutes on tithes and offerings. His covenant means an agreement between two or more persons to do or refrain from doing some act; a compact; a contract, in Biblical usage, the agreement or engagement of God with man as set forth in the Old and New Testament, a formal agreement of legal validity.

When God said in Malachi 3:8 "Will a man rob God? You are robbing Me, but you say, How have we robbed Thee?" Let God's inspired and infallible word answer this question, not

true

man's misguided ideas or his moral instructions.

The burnt offering is what God is saying He is being robbed of in Malachi 3:8.

The author of the Book of Hebrews identified Jesus as the great High Priest (Heb. 9:11) who replaced the system of animal sacrifices, a once and for all sacrifice of Himself (Heb. 9:12-28.) In light of Christ's full and final offering of sin, Paul urged Christians to present their bodies a living and holy sacrifice. (Rom. 12:1)

Ref. Through the Bible in 55 Minutes, Leviticus; the third book in the Bible takes its name from the tribe of Levi, descendants of one of Jacob's twelve sons. This tribe had been chosen by God to have charge of the sacred things and, from it came the priests. Later, when the nation was established, this tribe was responsible for the temple — its service, its music, its sacrifice, offerings, everything that had to do with the temple worship and upkeep.

This book of Leviticus, also written by Moses, gives detailed instructions and descriptions of the special offerings that were prescribed for the feast, ceremonies, and rituals. These offerings and sacrifices pointed forward to Christ, the true sacrifice, offering for sin. They were the shadow cast backward through the centuries by the cross; "the shadow of things to come," about which the Apostle Paul spoke in Col. 2:17.

Ref. King James Version, page 21 of the Bible. God is saying what offerings were and what they were used for. In the Old Testament we find offerings of (1)Meats (Meals), consisting of unleavened bread, cake, wafer, or grain mixed with salts, and except when a sin offering, with olive oil (Lev. 16:5-11 and 6:14-23, Num. 15:4,6,9). Sometimes accepted from the poor as a sin offering in place of the burnt offering Lev. 5: 3,11 (2)Drink consisting of wine and used with meat and burnt offerings, except in the sin and trespass offerings (Num 6:17 and 15:5, 10). (3) Animals, or sacrifice, cattle, sheep, and goats that were free from blemish (Lev. 1:3). These were of three kinds: (a)The burnt offering in which a male lamb, ram, goat, bullock, dove, or pigeon was entirely consumed on the altar (Lev. 1:1-17 and 6:9-13). (b) The sin offering in which a bullock, a male or female goat, a female lamb, a dove, or a pigeon was given (Lev. 4:1-35 and 6:25-30) and (c) The trespass offering in which a ram or a male lamb was used. (Lev. 5:1-19; 6:6,7; 7:1-8; 14:12, 21). (d) The peace offering, including the giving of thanks (Lev. 7:12-15), the payment of a vow (Ex. 35: 27-29; Lev. 7:16; Num. 6: 10-21), and the voluntary or freewill offering, (Lev. 7:16-20); for these any animal without blemish of either sex could be used, but no birds (Lev. 3:1-17; 7:11-27). In sacrifices, the term wave offering is used of those portions consecrated to the Lord by the rite of waving (Lev. 7: 7, 30-34; Num. 6:17-20), and the heave offering is used of those portions taken away and set apart for the Lord. (Lev. 7:14, 32-34; 18:9-32.) These were the offerings God said He was being robbed of.

Gen. 8-20 "Then Noah built an altar to God.

Gen. 8-21 "And the Lord smelled the soothing, aroma, and the Lord said to Himself. I will never again curse the ground on account of man, for the intent of man's heart is evil from his youth and I will never again destroy every living thing, as I have done."

Ref. The New Open Bible, New American Standard, page 377 - The altar Noah built was a platform or elevated place on which a priest placed a sacrifice as an offering to God. The Hebrew word for altar means a place of slaughter of sacrifice, but the altars of the Old Testament were not limited to sacrificial purposes. Sometimes an altar was built as a testimony of one's faith for future generations.

The burnt offering Noah offered symbolized the worshipper's desire to be purged of sinful acts. This is what God said He was being robbed of. Ref. Smith Bible Dic. Page 99.

What Noah did was to offer a sacrifice of the life of a person or an animal in payment for his sins.

God says the same thing in Lev.3:11 that He is saying in Lev. 1:3. But only the offering is different in Lev.1:3. The word 'offering' is applied to the offering, which was wholly consumed by fire on the altar, the whole of which, except the refuse ashes, ascended in smoke to God. The meaning of the whole burnt offering was that which is the original idea of all sacrifice, the offering of Himself, soul, and body, to God.

This is what God said offering was in Malachi 3:8, Ex. 29:18 "And you shall offer up in smoke the whole ram on the altar, it is a burnt offering to the Lord, it is a soothing aroma, an offering by fire to the Lord."

Ex. 29:27 "And you shall consecrate the breast of the wave offering and the thigh of the heave offering which was waved and which was offered from the ram or ordination from the one which was for Aaron and from the one which was his son."

Ex. 29:27 - Wave offering, Ref. Smith Bible Dic. Page 737 - This rite, together with that of heaving or raising the offering, was an inseparable accompaniment of peace offering. In such the right shoulder, considered the choicest part of the victim, was to be heaved, and viewed as holy to the Lord, only eaten therefore by the priest. The breast was to be waved, and eaten by the worshipper. The scriptural notices of these rites are to be found in Ex. 29:24; Lev. 7:30,34; Lev. 8:27, 9:21, 10:14, 15:23, 10:15-20; Num.6:20, 18:11,26-29, etc. In conjecturing the meaning of this rite, regard must be had that it was the accompaniment of peace offerings which were witnesses to a ratified covenant — an established communion between God and man. On the second day of the Passover feast, a sheaf of wheat and an unblemished lamb of the first year were waved.

God is saying that they robbed Him out of offering by offering animals that had defects and presenting Him with defiled food and blind sacrifice. Lame and sick animals were offered to Him. He said His offering must be without defect and unblemished, because He is Holy. This is why he said in Malachi 3:8 he was being robbed of offerings. They offer animals that were defective, lame, and sick. Many more scriptures in the Bible say that His offering must be without defect.

Both Old and New Testaments confirm that sacrifices were symbolic. Because of their sins, the Hebrews presented offerings by which they gave another life in place of their own. These substitutes of animal sacrifice pointed forward to the ultimate sacrifice of Jesus Christ. (Heb. 10:1-18), who laid down His life for the sins of all people.

Lev. Page 115. The blood offerings remind the worshippers that because of sin the Holy God requires the costly gift of life. The way to God is only through the blood sacrifice, and they can walk with God only through obedience to His Law.

This is what God is saying. He was being robbed of in Malachi 3:8. He is not saying an offering was money. There is not but one scripture in the Bible in which God said anything about an offering being money which was a contribution raising money, it was for the building of the Tabernacle, Ex. 25:1-7. He said to Moses to tell the sons of Israel to raise a contribution of gold, silver, and bronze. Here is what God said about offering in Heb.13:11. "For the bodies of those animals whose blood is brought into the Holy place by the High Priest as an offering for sin are burned outside the camp."

The material substance of sacrifice represented this great atonement as already made and accepted in God's foreknowledge. To those who grasped the ideas of sin, pardon, and self-dedication symbolized in them, they were means of entering into the blessing which the one true sacrifice alone procured. They could convey nothing in themselves, yet as types they might, if accepted by a true though necessarily imperfect faith, be means of conveying in some degree the blessings of the antitype. It is clear that the atonement in the Epistle to the Hebrews, as in the New Testament generally, is viewed in a two-fold light. On the one hand it is set forth distinctly as a vicarious sacrifice which was rendered necessary by the sin of man, and in which the Lord bore the sins of many. It is its essential characteristic that in it He stands absolutely alone offering His sacrifice without any reference to the faith or conversion of men. In it He stands out alone as the mediator between God and man, and His sacrifice is offered once for all, never to be imitated or repeated. Now this view of the atonement is set forth in the Epistle as typified by the sin offering. On the other hand the sacrifice of Christ is set forth to us as the completion of that perfect obedience to the will of the Father, which is the natural duty of sinless man. The main idea of this view of the atonement is it is representative rather than vicarious. It is typified by the burnt offering, Ref. Smith. Bible Dic. Page 578-579.

Ref. Smith Bible Dic. Page 578 - From the prophets and the Epistle to the Hebrews we learn that the sin offering represented that covenant as broken by man and as knit together again, by God's appointment through the shedding of blood. The shedding of the blood, the symbol of life, signified that the death of the offender was deserved for sin, but that the death of the victim was accepted for His death by the ordinance of God's mercy. Beyond all doubt the sin offering distinctly witnessed that sin existed in man, that the wages of that sin was death, and that God had provided atonement by the vicarious suffering of an appointed victim.

Christ Himself is the satisfying sacrifice for sins. The New Testament concept of propitiation is not at all like the pagan idea of appeasing a cruel deity that propitiation in the New

Testament is a result of God's love 1 John 4:10 occurs three times once meaning the Mercy seat (hilasterion), once meaning the cover of the ark of the covenant (Heb 9:5), and once translated the same as hilasmas. The mercy seat is the place where propitiation is made. Like so much in the Tabernacles, it pictured Christ and His work on the cross. The main teaching of these three terms is that not only is God satisfied with the person and work of His Son, but through faith in Him, we can be reconciled to God.

Many people who have studied Greek think the King James translators were in error in Romans 5:11 — when they had Paul write, "by whom we have now received the atonement." (Katallage) The standard Greek word for reconciliation, Atonement, today at least refers to the entire work that Christ performed on the cross. Actually, the K.J.V. scholars, brilliant linguists that they were, did choose the right word for 1611. In 1611, atonement meant at-one ment, that is coming from a position of enmity to one of friendship, becoming at one with each other. That is what reconciliation is.

Annual atonement was on the 10th day of the 7th month, the most solemn day of the year. The removal of sin was only for a year, (Heb. 10:3) But in those sacrifices, there is a reminder of sins year by year, but they pointed forward to eternal removal. (Zechariah 3:4, 8:9, 13:1) By God's foreknowledge, he foreordained our Lord as a sacrifice slain before the foundation of the World. Through faith in Him, we can be reconciled to God. Heb. 10:14 — For by one sacrifice, He has perfected for all time those who are sanctified. Ref. Halley Bible Handbook, page 136.

Scapegoat is translated in (R.V.) Azazel, which is thought to have been named for Satan. After the sacrificial goat had been offered, then the High Priest laid his hands on the head of the goat for Azazel, and confessed over him the sins of the people. Then the goat was led away into a solitary land, bearing away the sins of the people. This ceremony was one of God's historical fore-pictures of the coming atonement for human sin by the Death of Christ.

Ref. Smith. Bible Dic. page 839 — Some of the ceremonies which took place on the great Day of Atonement. Aaron, the High Priest, made sin-offering for himself and for the people, and sprinkled the blood upon the Mercy-Seat in the most Holy place, confessed the sins of the people over the scapegoat, and sent it away into the wilderness, and offered burnt offering for himself and for the people.

Ref. Smith. Bible Dic. Page 839 — Jesus Christ suffered in our place the punishment of our sins. The scapegoat bore the sins of Israel, as Christ bears ours. How must more shall the blood of Christ, who through the eternal Spirit offered Himself without spot to God, purge our conscience from dead works to serve the living God (Heb. 9:14)

Ref. Smith Bible Dic. Page 633-634 — sin offering. The sin offering among the Jews was sacrificed in which the ideas of propitiation and of atonement for sin most distinctly marked. The ceremonial of the sin offering is described in Lev. 4 and 6. The trespass offering is closely connected with the sin offering in Leviticus, but at the same time, clearly distinguished from it being in some cases offered with it as a distinct part of the same sacrifice as for example, in the cleansing of the leper, Lev. 14. The distinction of ceremonial clearly indicates a difference in the idea of the two sacrifices. The nature of that difference is still a subject of great controversy. We find that the sin offerings were (1) Regular (2) For the whole people, at the New Moon, Passover, Pentecost, Feast of Trumpets and Feast of Tabernacles, Num. 28:15; 29:38; besides the solemn offering of the two goats on the Great Day of Atonement. Lev. 16. For the priests and Levites at their consecration, Ex. 29:10; 14:36; besides the yearly sin offering (a bullock) for the high priest on the Great Day of Atonement. Lev. 16:2. Special for any "sin of ignorance" and like, recorded in Lev. 4 and 5. It is seen that in the law most of the sins which are not purely ceremonial are called sins of "ignorance," see Heb. 9:7; and in Num.15:30, it is expressly said that which such sins can be atoned for by offerings, the soul that doeth aught presumptuously (Heb. "with a high hand") "shall be cut off from among his people." "His iniquity shall be upon him." Comp. Heb. 10:26. But here are sufficient indications that the sins here called of "ignorance" are more strictly those of negligence or frailty, "repented of by the unpunished offender, as opposed to those of deliberate and unrepentant sin. It is clear that the two classes of sacrifices, although distinct, touch closely upon each other. It is also evident that the sin offering was the only regular and general recognition of sin in the abstract, and accordingly was far more solemn and symbolical in its ceremonial; the trespass offering was confined to special cases, most of which related to the doing of some material damage, either to the holy things or to man. Josephus declares that the sin offering is presented by those "who fall into sin in ignorance," and the trespass offering by "one who has sinned and is conscious of his sin, but has no one to convict him thereof." Without attempting to decide so difficult and so controverted a question, we may draw the following conclusions: first that the sin offering was far the more solemn and comprehensive of the two sacrifices. Secondly, that the sin offering looked more to the guilt of sin done irrespective of its consequences, while the trespass offering looked to the evil consequences of sin, either against the service of God or against man, and toward the duty of atonement, as far as atonement was possible. Third, that in the sin offering especially we find symbolized the acknowledgment of sinfulness as inherent in man, and of the need of expiation by sacrifice to renew the broken covenant between man and God. In considering this subject, it must be remembered that the sacrifices of the law had a temporal as well as a spiritual significance and effect. They restored an offender to his place in the commonwealth of Israel; they were therefore an atonement to the King of Israel for the infringement of his law. Infringement means to break, as law or contract; to violate; to transgress; to impair or encroach on.

✳ When God said he was being robbed of tithes and offerings, here is who He was speaking to. He said in Heb. 7:5 — who He called to take tithes, were the Levites, who received the office of the priesthood and had a commandment to take tithes of the people according to the Law that is of their brethren, their brethren is of the twelve tribes of Israel. This does not pertain to us. In Eph. 2:12 "Ye, (meaning us) were without Christ being aliens from the commonwealth of Israel, and strangers from the covenants of promise, having no hope and without God in the World, at that time."

✳ He is saying in Num. 18:26 — that He has given the tithes to the Levites for their inheritance, but He said for them to present Him an offering from the tithes, a tenth of the tithes as an offering. The scripture says in Num. 18:26 that offering came out of tithes. 2Chron. 31:5-6 — And as soon as the order spread, the sons of Israel provided in abundance the first fruits of grain, new wine, oil, honey and of all the produce of the field; and they brought in abundantly their tithes of all. (6) And the sons of Israel and Judah who lived in the cities of Judah also brought in the tithes of oxen and sheep, and the tithes of sacred gifts which were consecrated to the Lord their God, and placed them in heaps. Deu. 14:23 "And you shall eat in the presence of the Lord your God, at the place where He chooses to establish His name, the tithe of your grain, your new wine, your oil, and the first-born of your herd and your flock, in order that you may learn to fear the Lord your God always." Neh. 10:36 "And bring to the house of God the first-born of our herds and our flocks as it is written in the law, for the priests who are ministering in the house of our God." (38) "And the priest, the son of Aaron, shall be with the

Levites when the Levites receive tithes, and the Levites shall bring up the tenth of the tithes to the house of our god to the chamber of the storehouse."
Now you have read from the scriptures that offerings and tithes were animals and many other things, like grain, oil, new wine, and what came out of the field, in Deu. 14:22. The scripture says in 2Chron. 31:6 — tithes were sacred gifts (not money). In Neh. 10:36 tithes were under the law as it is written. ⟩

But many Churches are teaching God's word that we are robbing God of tithes and offerings if we don't pay our tithes and offerings. They are teaching false doctrine. This is what our Churches and Pastors are doing by their ungodly, wicked, unrighteousness. Tithes were under the Law. In Heb. 8:13 a new covenant has made the first obsolete. Obsolete means growing old, ready to disappear. We were never under the Law, only the nation of Israel was.

Meat offering — The law or ceremonial of the meat is the offering described in Lev. 2 and 6:14-23. It was to be composed of fine flour, seasoned with salt and mixed with oil and frankincense, but without leaven; and it was generally accompanied by a drink offering of wine. A portion of it, including all frankincense, was to be burnt on the altar as a memorial; the rest belonged to the priests; but the meat offering offered by the priests themselves was to be burnt. Its meaning appears to be exactly expressed in the word of David. 1Chron. 29:10-14. It will be seen that this meaning involves neither of the main ideas of sacrifice — neither the atonement for sin nor self-dedication to God. It takes them for granted, and is based on them. Rather it expresses gratitude and love to God as the giver of all. Accordingly the meat offering, properly so called, seems always to have been a subsidiary offering, needing to be introduced by the sin offering, which represented the one idea, and to have formed an appendage to the burnt offering, which represented the other. The unbloody offerings offered alone did not properly belong to the regular meat offering; they were usually substitutes for other offerings. Ref. Smith Bible Dic. Page 390.

Ref. New Open bible New American Standard page, 115 - The meat or meal offering typifies Christ's sinless service. Halleys Bible Handbook, page 135 - The Levitical Priesthood was divinely ordained as mediator between God and the Hebrew nation in the ministry of animal sacrifice. These sacrifices were fulfilled in Christ. Animal sacrifices are no longer necessary. Christ Himself is the Great High-Priest for man; the Only Mediator between God and man. (Heb. 8:9-10)

Ref. Halleys Bible Handbook, page 653. Sins removed forever. No need for further sacrifice. Christ's death is entirely sufficient to take care of all previous sins, and those that in weakness we may in daily life commit. God can now Forgive, and will Forgive, those who place their Trust in Christ.

Sacrifice was a ritual through which Hebrew people offered the blood or flesh of an animal to God in payment for their sins. Sacrifice originated in the Garden of Eden, when God killed animals and made tunics for Adam and Eve (Gen. 3:21). God's provision of this covering symbolized that sinful man could come before God without fear of death.

When Noah left the ark, his first act was to build an altar and sacrifice, offering animals to God (Gen. 8:20). Abraham regularly worshipped God by offering sacrifice to Him (Gen. 2:7).

Both Old and New Testaments confirm that sacrifices were symbolic. Because of their sins, the Hebrews presented sacrifices by which they gave another life in place of their own. These animal substitutes were offered to God for the sins of the people of Israel.

Ref. New Open Bible New American Standard, page 119. Old Testament offerings. The patriarchs of the Old Testament — Abraham, Isaac, and Jacob - built altars and made sacrifices to God wherever they settled (Gen12:8, 26:25, 28:18.) Cain and Abel made the first offering to God, the offering Abel made was of the firstlings of his flock, his flock was his animal offered to God, which He sanctified in Num. 3:13, and in Ex. 13:2.

The author of the Book of Hebrews identified Jesus as the great High Priest (Heb. 9:11) who replaced the system of animal sacrifices, with a once-for-all sacrifice of Himself (Heb. 9:12-28). In the light of Christ's full and final offering for sin, Paul urged Christians to present their bodies as a living and holy sacrifice. (Rom. 12:1).

(1) (A). Origin of Sacrifice. The universal prevalence of sacrifice shows it to have been primeval, and deeply rooted in the instincts of humanity. Whether it was first enjoined by an external command, or whether it was based on that sense of sin and lost communion with God which is stamped by his hand on the heart of man, is a historical question which cannot be determined. (B) Ante-Mosaic History of Sacrifice.

In examining the various sacrifices, Ref. Smith Bible Dic. Page 577 says offering was a sacrifice recorded in Scripture before the establishment of the law. We find that the words specially denoting expiatory sacrifice are not applied to them. This fact does not at all show that they were not actually expiatory, but it justifies the inference that this idea was not actually the prominent one in the doctrine of sacrifice. The sacrifices of Cain and Abel are called minchah, and appear to have been eucharistic. Noah's (Gen. 8:20) and Jacob's at Mizpah, were at the institution of a covenant, and may be called federative. In the burnt offerings of Job for his children (Job 1:5), and for his three friends (Job 41:8), we for the first time find the expression of the desire of expiation. The same is the case in the words of Moses to Pharaoh, (Ex 10:25). Here the main idea is at least deprecatory. (C) The sacrifices or offerings of the Mosaic Period. These are inaugurated by the offering of The Passover and the sacrifice of Ex. 24. The Passover indeed is unique in its character; but it is clear that the idea of salvation from death means of sacrifice is brought out in it with a distinctness before unknown. The law of Leviticus now unfolds distinctly the various forms of sacrifice. (A) The burnt offering, self-dedicatory; (B) the meat offering (Unbloody); Eucharistic. (C) the peace offering (bloody). Eucharistic means Thanksgiving, the Lords Supper, eucharistos, grateful. The Christian sacrament of the Lords Supper; the Holy Communion; the consecrated elements of bread and wine. (C) The sin offering; the trespass offering; Expiatory. (D) The incense offered after sacrifice in the holy place, and on the Day of Atonement in the holy of holies, the symbol of the intercession of the priest (as a type of great High Priest), accompanying and making efficacious the prayers of the people. In the consecration of Aaron and his sons, Lev. 8, we find these offered in what became ever afterward their appointed order. First came the sin offering, to prepare access to God; next the burnt offering, to mark their dedication to his service; and third the meat offering of thanksgiving. Henceforth the sacrificial system was fixed in all its parts until he should come whom it typified. (D) Post-Mosaic Sacrifices, - It will not be necessary to pursue, in detail, the history of the post-Mosaic sacrifice, for its main principles were now fixed forever. The regular sacrifices, in the temple services, were (A) Burnt offerings. 1. The daily burnt offerings Ex. 29:38-42, the double burnt offerings on the Sabbath, Num. 28:9, 10:3, the burnt offerings at the great festivals; Num. 28:11-29, 39. (B) Meat offerings. 1. The daily meat offerings accompanying the daily burnt offerings Ex. 29:40, 41:2, the shewbread, renewed every Sabbath, Lev. 24:5, 9:3, the special meat offerings at the Sabbath and the great festivals, Num. 28, 29:4, the first fruits, at the Passover, Lev. 23:10-14 at Pentecost, Lev. 23:17-20, the first fruits of the dough and threshing-floor at the harvest time. Num. 15:20-21; Deu. 26:1-11. (C) Sin offerings 1. Sin offering each new moon. Num. 28:15, 2, sin offering at the Passover, Pentecost, Feast of the Trumpets and Tabernacles, Num. 28:22, 30:29, 5:16, 19, 22, 25, 28, 31, 34, 38:3, the offering of the two goats for the people and of the bullock for the priest himself, on the Great Day of Atonement. Lev.16. (D) Incense. 1. The morning and evening incense, Ex. 30:7, 8:2, the incense of the Great Day of Atonement. Lev. 16:12. Besides these public sacrifices, there were offerings of the people for themselves individually.

11. By the order of sacrifices in its perfect form, as in Lev. 8, it is clear that the sin offering occupies the most important place; the burnt offering comes next, and the meat offering or peace offering last of all. The second could only be offered after the first had been accepted, the third was only a subsidiary part of the second. Yet, in actual order or time, it has been that the patriarchal sacrifices partook much more of the nature of the peace offering and burnt offering, and that under the law, by which was "the knowledge of sin," Rom. 3:20.

The sin offering was for the first time explicitly set forth. This is but natural, that the deepest ideas should be the last in order of development. The essential difference between heathen views of sacrifice and the scriptural doctrine of the Old Testament is not to be found in its denial of any of these views. In fact, it brings out clearly and distinctly the ideas which in heathenism were uncertain, vague and perverted. But the essential points of distinction are two. First, that whereas the heathen conceived of their gods as alienated in jealously or anger, to be sought after and to be appeased by the unaided action of man, scripture represents God Himself as approaching man, as pointing out and sanctioning the way by which the broken covenant should be restored. The second mark of distinction is closely connected with this inasmuch as it shows sacrifice of animals to be a scheme proceeding from God, and in His foreknowledge connected with the one central fact of all human history. Page 578, Smith Bible Dic.

Page 578 Smith Bible Dic. From the prophets, and the Epistle to the Hebrews, we learn that the sin offering represented Christ's sacrifice as our expiation and our atonement for sins. The shedding of the blood, the symbol of life, signified that the death of the offender was deserved for sin, but that the death by the victim was accepted for his death by the ordinances of God. Beyond all doubt the sin offering distinctly witnessed that sin existed in man, that the "wages of sin was death," and that God had provided an atonement. This is what the sin offering represented and foreshadowed Christ as our atonement sacrifice for our sins.

In Malachi 3:8-10 - When God said He was being robbed of offerings, our Church Pastors are lying about this scripture, by saying God is saying offerings are money. Well, God is not a man that He should LIE. He cannot be a true God, and contradict Himself. God and His Spirit agree with His Inspired infallible Holy word, on what offering He was robbed of. Tithes are not money.

Chapter 8

These are scriptures used by the Seven-Day Adventist Church, and some Baptist Churches, and the Church of God and Christ and many other churches to misleading us about tithes and offerings.

2Tim. 4:4 "And they shall turn away their ears from the truth, and shall be turned unto a fable." They won't listen to what the Bible says, but will blithely follow their own misguided ideas.

In 2Tim 4:4 God is speaking to us today, that His Word is Spiritual truth. His Inspired Word is infallible, trustworthy, not liable to error on doctrine. His Word lasts through eternity, Pastor, on what tithes and offerings were, but you will turn your ears from the truth.

God is saying in 2Tim 4:4 - To His Church, and their Pastor who He asks to shepherd and oversee His Flock, not under compulsion, but voluntarily, according to the will of God, and not for sordid gain, but with the eagerness, but they won't listen to what the Bible says, but will blithely follow their own misguided ideas like turning what His Inspired infallible word says what tithes are, to change His word to a fable, for the love of MONEY.

1Timothy says "for the love of money is the root of all evil which while some coveted after, they have erred from the faith, and pierced themselves through with many sorrow." But Pastor, people long to be rich soon begin to do all kinds of wrong things like teaching tithes are money, which is so false. By teaching false doctrine will hurt them and make them evil-minded and finally send them to HELL itself. For the love of money is the first step toward all kinds of sin. Some people, Pastor, have even turned away from God's Inspired infallible word to teach a false doctrine about tithes being money, because of their love for money, and as a result have pierced themselves with many sorrows. Oh, Timothy, you are God's man, Pastor, run from all evil things and work instead at what is right and good, learning to trust in Him and love others, and be patient and gentle. If you as a Pastor love your members, why not stop lying to them about tithes being money? Don't you, Pastor, have faith in your God, that you don't have to lie about Him to say He called you to take tithes? This is, of all the sins against God, the most serious, that of self-will. This sin led to the fall of Satan. (Is. 14:12-14) and it can be said to be the root of Adam's transgression (Gen. 3:1-7). It is therefore, of utmost importance that we, Pastor, that we as the children of God find His will and perform it. Pastor, God said without faith it is impossible to please Him. Have all Pastors lost their faith in God? When God said that He shall supply all your needs according to His riches in glory by Christ Jesus. If it is money, God said He would supply it, put your faith in your God, and stop lying about His word about tithes being money! Fight on for God. Hold tightly to the eternal life which God has given you, and which you have confessed with such a ringing confession before many witnesses. Because God is not a man that He should lie about tithes being money. Also, the word of God and the spirit of God agree in all things pertaining to His word. For He cannot be a true God and contradict Himself. The word of God is absolutely reliable and true, it is His infallible inspired Holy word. God is not a God of confusion. He wouldn't say to pay Him tithes, a tenth of our money. He cannot accept anything that He hasn't sanctified or consecrated to be free from sin and undefiled.

In His holy bible, there are scriptures on giving, 2Cor. 9:7-15; 1Cor. 16:1,2; Luke 6:38. These were scriptures God put in His word on giving. It would be confusing if He said to pay tithes, and then put these scriptures in His word. He is not a God of confusion. If we as Christians would only begin to do as Paul said (in 2 Tim. 2:15) we would surely learn and know what is true. (Acts 17:11) "Now these were more noble minded than those in Thessalonica, for they received the word with eagerness examining the Scriptures daily to see whether these things were so." This is why Christians should study the scriptures daily, then we will find out for ourselves that our Pastors are teaching tithes being money, and that this is false. But God is saying today, to all his Pastors, He called to shepherd His flock, to return to His Word on what tithes were.

Here are those scriptures, used by the Seven-Day Adventist Church, the Baptist Church, and the Church of God and Christ, and many other Churches to mislead us about tithes: Lev. 27:30; Malachi 3:8-11. Matthew 23:23.

God says, in Col. 2:8, "See to it that no one takes you captive through philosophy and empty deception, according to the tradition of men, according to the elementary principles of the World, rather than according to Christ. Don't let others spoil your faith, and joy with their philosophies, their wrong and shallow answers built on men's thought and ideas, instead of on what Christ has said."

Rom. 1:18 - For the wrath of God is revealed from Heaven against all ungodliness and unrighteousness of men, Pastor, who suppress the truth in unrighteousness. Pastor, God said His wrath is revealed from heaven against all ungodliness, means - not godly, godless, wicked.

Our churches and their Pastors have taught us a system of beliefs for four hundred years, about tithes and offerings being money. For four hundred years, our churches and their Pastors have held us captive through doctrine, tradition, and by philosophy with their empty deception, misleading us by principles of the world's doctrine and by their wrong and shallow answers built on men's thought and ideas, rather than according to what God says. They have suppressed this truth by not revealing to you that the Scripture says there is no difference between tithes and offerings. They are the same thing.

God is saying the same thing He said to the nation of Israel. Pastor, you have turned aside from My word by teaching your own doctrine on tithes and offering being money. Not one Pastor did He call, Heb. 7:5 and His son ended the Law, in Rom. 10:4 — tithes are no longer. "For we brought nothing into this world, and it is certain we can carry nothing out." 1Tim. 6:9 — But people who long to be rich soon begin to do all kinds of wrong things to get money, things that hurt them and make them evil-minded and finally send them to Hell itself. 1Tim. 6:5 — These arguers, their minds, warped by sin, don't know how to tell the truth about tithes or offerings, to them the Good News is just a means of making money; keep away from them. 1 Tim. 6:11 - "But flee from these things, you man of God; and pursue righteousness, godliness, faith, love, perseverance, and gentleness. (12) Fight the good fight of faith, take hold of the eternal life to which you were called."

Our churches Pastors don't reveal the truth about Mal. 3:9 — They suppress this truth by not revealing to their church members what nation God said was robbing Him, suggesting we were the nation that He was speaking about. We were heathens, a nation that worshipped idols at that time in the world, and without God. Eph. 2:12.

Our churches Pastors use this scripture, Mal. 3:9, to put fear in us by saying if we don't pay our tithes and offerings that we are cursed with a curse. "For this nation is robbing Me, the whole nation of you. When God said that, He was not saying this nation we live in today.

All nations worshipped idols. There were gods everywhere: gods of the sky, gods of the earth, gods of the sea, gods of the land, gods of the cities, gods of the country, gods of the mountains, gods of the valleys, male gods, female gods, families of gods. Ref. Halleys Bible Handbook, page 31. All nations worshipped gods as Dagon (the fish god), Molech (Kings), fire god-Ball (lord), Asherah (straight) name of phoenician gods - Ashtaroth (star). Ref. Smith Bible Dic. Page, 59.

The Old Testament is an account of God's age-long effort to establish, in a world of idol-worshipping nations, the idea that there is One God by building a nation around this idea. God's ultimate objective was to bring Christ into the world; God's immediate objective was to establish, in a world of Idolatry, as a background to the coming of Christ, the idea that there is One True Living God. Ref. Halleys Bible Handbook, page 31.

Here starts the story of Redemption. It had been hinted at in the Garden of Eden (3:15). Now, 2000 years after the creation and fall of Man, 400 years after the Flood, in a world lapsed into idolatry and wickedness, God called Abraham to become the founder of the movement, having for its object the Reclamation and Redemption of Mankind.

In that pioneer age of the earth, while nations were still not much more than tribal communities, setting the more favored lands, Abraham was a righteous man, a believer in God, not an idolater, one of the few still holding to the tradition of primitive Monotheism. Monotheism the doctrine of, or belief in, the existence of one God only. God promised that his descendants that:

71

(1) They should become a great nation. This is the nation that God said robbed Him out of tithes and offerings, the nation that came from Abraham's descendants, the Nation of Israel. All nations were heathen, they were idol worshipers, Abraham's descendants. "And you shall be to Me a kingdom of Priests and a holy Nation. (2) You should inherit the land of Canaan. (3) Through you all nations should be blessed." We are blessed because those sacrificial offerings the Priest offered to God pointed forward to Christ, the infinite sacrifice for sin. Those sacrifices were fulfilled in Christ. Animal sacrifices are no longer necessary. The priest offered the blood of animals. Christ offered His own blood. Once and for all, when God said all Nations should be blessed through Abraham's descendants, we were blessed because Christ came through the Tribe of Judah, they were Abraham descendants.

This promise in Genesis (12:2, 3:22, 18) is the foundation of which the whole Bible is a development, God first called Abraham in Ur (Acts 7:2-4); (Genesis 11:31), again in Haran (12:1-4), again in Shechem (12:7), again in Bethel (13:14-17). And twice in Hebron (15:5,18; 17:1-8). The promise was repeated to Isaac (26:3,4). And to Jacob (Genesis 28:13, 14; 35:11,12; 46: 3,4)

Abraham was not an idolater; His countrymen were idolaters. But, he lived in a world of idolatry. In the beginning, man had One God; and in the Garden of Eden, he had lived in rather intimate communion with God. But with his sin and banishment, man lost his primeval knowledge of God; and, groping in his darkness for a solution to the mysteries of existence, he came to worship the powers of Nature which seem to him to be the source of life. Sex, because it was the means through which life came, played a very important part in early Babylonian religion. Cuneiform inscriptions have revealed that a large part of their liturgies were descriptions of sexual intercourse between gods and goddesses, through which, they thought, all things came into being. Then, too, the Sun and Rain and various forces of nature were deified, because on them depended the life of the world. And Kings also, because they had power, came to be deified. Many cities and nations had for their chief god their founder: as Asshu, father of the Assyrians, became the chief god of the Assyrians; and Marduck, Nimrod, founder of Babylon, became the chief god of Babylon. And, to make their gods more real, images were made to represent the gods; and then the images themselves came to be worshipped as gods. Thus, man took his nose-dive from Original Monotheism into the abyss of innumerable polytheistic idolatrous cultures, some of which, in their practices, were unspeakably vile and abominable. Ref. Halley Bible Handbook, page 95.

Ref. Halley Bible Handbook, page 95 - In Abraham's day, Ur was in Babylonia, and Babylonians had many goddesses. They were worshipers of fire, the sun, moon, stars and various forces of nature. Nimrod, who had exalted himself against God in building the Tower of Babel, was ever afterward recognized as the Chief Babylonian deity. Marduk was the common form of his name; later it became identical with Bel. Shamash was the name of the sun-god. Sin, the moon-god was the principal deity of Ur, Abraham's city. Sin's wife was called Ningal, the moon - goddess of Ur. She had many names, and was worshipped in every city as the Mother-Goddess. Nina was one of her names, from which the city of Nineveh was named. Her commonest name in Babylonia was Ishtar. She was the deification of sexual passion; her worship required licentiousness. Sacred prostitution in connection with her sanctuaries was a universal custom among the women of Babylonia. Her temples were charming retreats or chambers where her priestesses entertained male worshipers in disgraceful ceremonies. In addition to these prostitute priestesses, every maid, wife or widow had to officiate at least once in her lifetime in these rites.

Abraham believed in One God. His countrymen were idolaters. His father was an idolater (Joshua 24:2). There are legends of his being persecuted as a child for refusal to worship idols. How did Abraham know about God? No doubt, by direct revelation from God. And moreover, taking the figures in chapters (5) and (11) as they are. Noah's life extended to the birth of Abraham; and Noah's life was overlapped by Methuselah's by 600 years. While Methuselah's life was overlapped by Adam's by 243 years. So Abraham could have learned directly from Shem, Noah's account of the Flood and Methuselah's account of Adam and the Garden of Eden. (Ref. Halley's Bible Handbook, page 95).

When God said in Mal. 3:9 "You are cursed with a curse, for you are robbing Me, this whole nation of you." When God said that we were Gentiles, heathens. We were worshipers of Idols, in the world without God. Ephesians 2:11 "Wherefore remember, that ye being in time past Gentiles in the flesh, who are called uncircumcised by that which is called the Circumcision in the flesh made by hands." When God said that, we were in the world without God. All nations were heathen. We as Gentiles served not the God of this world. We had no hope, and were without God in the world. Remember we were Gentiles, were living utterly apart from God. We were enemies of God's children and He promised us no help. Ex. 19:5-8 "Now then, if you will indeed obey My voice and keep My covenant, then you shall be My own possession among all the peoples, for all the earth is Mine. (6) and you shall be to Me a kingdom of priests and a holy nation." God is speaking about the nation of Israel as His Holy Nation. The only nation and God said was His was the nation of Israel. All other nations were heathen and worshipped idols. So Moses came and called the elders of the people, and set before them all these words which the Lord had commanded him, (8) "And all the people answered together and said, "All that the Lord has spoken we will do." And Moses brought back the words of the people to the Lord.

Rom. 10:4 says Christ is the end of the Law, which tithes and offerings came under. Gal. 3:1-29 — Therefore the Law has become our tutor to lead us to Christ. (Gal. 3:13) Christ redeemed us from the curse of the Law, having become a curse for us for it is written. "Cursed is everyone who hangs on a Tree." Eph. 2:15-20. Christ abolished His flesh the Enmity, which is the Law of commandments contained in ordinances that Himself He might make the two into one new man, thus establishing peace. Gen. 12:1 — Now the Lord said to Abram "Go forth from your country, and from your relatives, and from your father's house, to the land which I will show you." Gen. 12:2 "and I will make you a great nation, and I will bless you, and make your name great; and so you shall be a blessing." Gen. 12:3 "and I will bless those who bless you, and the one who curses you I will curse, and in you all the families of the earth shall be blessed." Gen. 13:1-6 "And I will make your descendants as the dust of the earth; so that if anyone can number the dust of the earth, then your descendants can also be numbered." Gen. 15. One of the most mysterious and yet theologically significant events is recorded in Gen. 15. In a vision, God told Abram to take a heifer, a goat, ram, a turtledove, and a young pigeon and cut all except the birds in half. Then he was told to place each piece opposite the other.

"Now when the sun was going down, a deep sleep fell upon Abram; and behold terror and great darkness fell upon him." (12). Then God predicted the 400-year bondage of Abram's descendants in a foreign land and their return to Canaan at the end of four generations.

"And it came about, when the sun had set, that it was very dark, and behold, there appeared a smoking oven and a flaming torch which passed between these pieces. On that day the Lord made (Heb.karat.lit.cut) a covenant (Heb.berit) with Abram (17,18). Then followed the prediction of the extent of the land to be given to Abram's descendants.

The Hebrew idiom "cutting a covenant" was based o the custom of cutting up an animal, and those who were making the covenant walked between the pieces. In this case, only God (visualized as a smoking oven and a flaming torch) went through. This suggest to many that it was an unconditional covenant on God's part, no matter what Abram did or did not do.

Gen. 17:1 "Now when Abram was ninety-nine years old, the Lord appeared to Abram and said to him, I am God Almighty; walk before Me, and be blameless."

Gen. 17:2 "And I will establish My covenant between Me and you, And I will multiply you exceedingly.

Gen. 17:3 "And Abram fell on his face, and God talked with him, saying"

Gen. 17:4 "As for Me, Behold, My covenant is with you, And you shall be the father of a multitude of nations."

Covenant is a word with many shades of meaning, used for all sorts of formal agreements between people, or between God and man. Most important of all, a covenant between God and man, was "cut" with animal sacrifices, offerings, oaths, and promised blessings for obedience and curses for disobedience.

The Covenants and Bible Doctrine - All Bible-Believing Christians believe in the covenants, but some make them central to their theology and some see them as an important part of a larger framework.

Those who fit the whole Bible into a covenantal framework are known as covenant theologians. Those who see the covenants as within larger administrations (dispensations) are known as dispensationalists. Recently, conservative Christians from both groups have found out that they have much more in common than they previously thought. Whether one favors .

covenants or dispensations, or both, the main program is neither the one nor the other, but the Person of Christ, (who in all, all, and in all.) He is our New covenant, once and for all.

Gen. 17:5 "No longer shall your name be called Abram, But your name shall be Abraham; For I will make you the father of a multitude of nations."

Gen. 17:6 "And I will make you exceedingly fruitful, and I will make nations of you, and Kings shall come forth from you."

Gen. 17:7 "And I will establish My covenant between Me and you and your descendants after you throughout their generations for an everlasting covenant to be God to you and your descendants after you."

Gen. 17:1-27 "Now this is My covenant, which you shall keep, between Me and you and your descendants after you; every male among you shall be circumcised."

Gen. 22:1-24 "And the angel of the Lord called to Abraham a second time from Heaven."

Gen. 22:17 "Indeed I will greatly bless you, and I will greatly multiply your seed as the stars of the Heavens, and as the sand which is on the seashore; and your seed shall possess the gate of their enemies."

Gen. 22:18 "And in your seed shall all Nations of the earth be blessed because you have obeyed My voice."

Gen. 26:4 "And I will multiply your descendants as the stars of Heaven, and will give your descendants all these lands and by your descendants all the nations of the earth shall be blessed."

Gen. 26:5 "Because Abraham obeyed Me and kept My charge, My commandments, My statutes and My Laws."

Gen. 26:24 This is what the Lord said to Isaac (24). The promise was repeated to Isaac. "And the Lord appeared to him the same night and said, I am the God of your father Abraham; do not fear, for I am with you, I will bless you and multiply your descendants, For the sake of My servant Abraham."

Gen. 28:13 Now the promise was repeated to Jacob. "And behold, the Lord stood above it and said, I am the Lord, the God of your father Abraham and the God of Isaac; the land on which thou liest, I will give it to you and your descendants."

Gen. 28:14 "Your descendants shall also be like the dust of the earth, and you shall spread out to the west and the east and to the north and to the south, and in you and in your descendants shall all the families of the earth be blessed."

Gen. 35:10 "And God said to him, Your name is Jacob; You shall no longer be called Jacob, But Israel shall be your name. Thus He called him Israel."

Gen. 35:11 "God also said to him, I am God Almighty; Be fruitful and multiply: A nation and company of Nations shall come forth from you and Kings shall come forth from you.

Gen. 35:12 "And the land which I gave to Abraham and Isaac, I will give it to you, And will give the land to your descendants after you."

Gen. 46:1 "So Israel set out with all that he had, and came to Beersheba, and offered sacrifices and offerings to the God of his father Isaac."

Gen. 46:2 "And God spoke to Israel in visions of the night and said, Jacob, Jacob. And he said, Here I am."

Gen. 46:3 "And He said, I am God, the God of your father; do not be afraid to go down to Egypt, for I will make you a great nation there."

Gen. 49; Read chapter 49 - about the names of the twelve tribes of Israel, the names of Jacob's twelve sons became the twelve tribes of Israel.

Gen. 49; "All these are the twelve tribes of Israel, and this is what their father said to them, when he blessed them. He blessed them, every one with the blessing appropriate to him, and according to his blessings."

Ex. 19:5 "Now then, if you will indeed obey My voice and keep My covenant, then you shall be My own possession among all the peoples, for all the earth is Mine."

Ex. 19:6 "And you shall be to Me a Kingdom of priests and a holy nation. These are the words that you shall speak to the sons of Israel."

Gen. 17:7 "and I will establish My covenant between Me and you and your descendants after you throughout their generations for an everlasting covenant, to be God to you and your descendants after you."

Gen. 35:10-11 - The nation God said He would make a great nation from Abraham's descendants, came through Jacob, whose name was changed from Jacob to Israel. God also said to Israel, "I am God Almighty. Be fruitful and multiply, a nation and company of nations shall come from you, and Kings shall come forth from you."

Gen. 46:3 And He said, "I am God, the god of your father, do not be afraid to go down to Egypt, for I will make you a great nation there."

Ex. 19:6 "and you shall be to Me a Kingdom of priests and a holy nation. These are the words that you shall speak to the sons of Israel." Pastor, whom He called to shepherd over His flock, Ye can not drink the cup of the Lord, and the cup of the Devil; Ye cannot be partakers of the Lord's table, and the table of Devils. God said in 2Tim. 4:4 - to His church members, also to you, Pastor, "And they shall turn away their ears from the truth, and shall be turned the truth unto a fable." They won't listen to what the Bible says but will blithely follow the misguided ideas. God said to you, Pastor, in 1Pet. 5:2 "To feed the flock of God which is among you, taking the oversight thereof, not by constraint, but willingly; not for filthy lucre, but of a ready mind." Pastor, filthy lucre is any money, Pastor, what are you doing when you as a Pastor ask or make a request to obtain or claim that God said for us to pay tithes and offerings, this is filthy lucre because tithes and offerings were not money. It is unrighteousness on your part, and deception, and misleading your church members by fraud, by deluding the truth for filthy lucre. 1Pet. 5:2 - God said Feed the flock of God; care for them willingly, not grudgingly; not for what you will get out of it, but because you are eager to serve the Lord.

All Scripture is inspired by God and is profitable for teaching, for reproof, for correction, for training in righteousness, not for man's guided ideals or his own doctrine or morals, about tithes, and offerings being money. For four hundred years these churches have suppressed the truth about what nation God said was robbing Him. They have suppressed this truth in their unrighteousness and by being ungodly, by capturing us in their own philosophy, by not revealing the truth about what nation God said was robbing Him out of tithes and offerings, or which nation was cursed with a curse.

God had foreknowledge that man would do this, turn away from the truth on what His Holy Inspired Infallible Word says and turned it into a fable. He also knew that they would teach a fable about tithes and offerings being Money. These are fables of false teachers claiming to belong to the Christian Church, but not possessing spiritual truth, speaking with human interests and passions. God, being Omniscient, all-knowing, he foretold that some Pastors would teach fables on His word about tithes and offerings being money. But He also said His wrath in Rom 1:18 is revealed from heaven against all ungodliness and unrighteousness of Men, Pastors who suppress His Truth in unrighteousness for the love of Money is filthy lucre, taken by you. A person makes deceitful pretenses, as some Pastors are doing by saying tithes and offerings were money God said he was being robbed of. Some Pastors that ask for tithes are false teachers and impostors. 1Pet. 5:2 - God is saying in this scripture, feed His flock, not for what you will get out of it, but with a ready mind, not for filthy lucre. This is what some of our Pastors are doing and have been doing for the last four hundred years, to turn God's word into a fable, by teaching tithes. This is on their own unrighteousness, and ungodliness, deluding the word of God by their deception on tithes.

Leviticus focuses on the worship and walk of the nation of God. In Exodus, Israel was redeemed and established as a Kingdom of priests and a holy nation. Leviticus shows how God's people are to fulfill their priestly calling.

The Hebrew title is (Wayyiqra), "And He called," the Talmud refers to Leviticus as the "Law of the Priests," and the Law of the offerings of animal sacrifice. The Greek title, appearing in the Deptaugint, is Leuitikom. "That which pertains to the Levites. From this word the Latin Vulgate derived its name Leviticus which was adopted as an English title. This title is slightly misleading because the book does not deal with the Leviticus as a whole, but more with the priests, a segment of the Levites. The Law of Offerings is in the Books of Leviticus, Numbers and Deuteronomy.

Keys to Leviticus: Holiness - Leviticus centers around the concept of the holiness of God, and how an unholy people can acceptably approach Him and then remain in continued fellowship. The way to God is only through blood sacrifice, the offering of animals to Him for their sins, and the walk with God is only through obedience to His Laws. Leviticus 17:11-20 "For the life of the flesh is in the blood and I have given it to you on the altar to make atonement for your souls; for it is the blood by reason of the life that makes atonement." (17:11)

Leviticus can also be called, "The Book of the Law of Priests" as it contains very little historical matter, concerning itself with priestly legislation and the practice of the Law among the people. Much importance is placed upon Israel's separation from heathen influences so that the nation may retain its religious purity. It was God's purpose to make the children of Israel His official representatives before the world, a Kingdom of priests, and a holy nation. Ex. 19:6. This tribe had been chosen by God to have a charge of the sacred things, and from this tribe came priests. This book of Leviticus, also written by Moses, gives detailed instructions and descriptions of the special offerings that were prescribed for the feasts, ceremonies, and rituals. These offerings and sacrifices pointed forward to Christ, the true sacrifice, offering for sin. They were the shadow cast backward through the centuries by the cross, the "shadow of things to come," about which the Apostle Paul spoke in Colossians 2:17.

Here is who God called to collect tithes, and later what tithes were, Ex. 28:1 "Then bring near to yourself Aaron your brother [God said to Moses], and his sons with him, from among the sons of Israel, to minister as priests to Me, Aaron, Nadab and Abihu, Eleazar and Ithamar, Aaron's sons."

Ref. Smith Bible. Dic., page 532 - The priesthood was first established in the family of Aaron, and all the sons of Aaron were priests. They stood between the high priest on one hand and the Levites on the other.

When the priesthood was instituted in the wilderness, Moses consecrated Aaron as the first high priest of Israel. The priesthood was set within the tribal of Levi from which Aaron was descended and Aaron's sons inherited the position of high priest from their father. Ref. New Open Bible New American Standard, page 99.

Same references, page 99 - The high priest's dress represented his function as mediator between God and people. Over his regular priestly garments the high priest wore an ephod, a two-piece apron. He also wore a breastpiece of judgment with twelve precious stones. These were engraved with the names of the twelve tribes of Israel, the names of the twelve sons of Jacob. In the pocket of the breastpiece, directly over the high priest's heart, were the Urim and Thummim (Ex. 28:30), the medium through which God communicated His will to the people. He must offer up their prayers, thanksgivings, sacrifice, offerings. He became their representative in "things pertaining unto God." The chief duties of the priests were to watch over the fire on the altar of burnt offering, and to keep it burning evermore both by day and night. They were also to teach the children of Israel the statues about provision for support. This consisted of (1) of one tenth of the tithes which the people paid to the Levites, one percent, on the whole produce of the field every year. Deu. 14:22, Num. 18:26-28, with a special tithe every third year. Deu. 14:28.

The high priest was responsible for seeing that the duties of the priest were carried out (2Chron. 19:11 His most important responsibility occurred annually on the Day of Atonement. On this day he entered the Holy of Holies, or the most Holy place in the tabernacle, and made sacrifices, offerings of animal first for his own sins, then for the sins committed by all the people during the year just ended (Ex. 30:10) Ref. New Open Bible New American Standard, page 99.)

The word "Leviticus" means "pertaining to Levites"; that is the book contains the System of Laws, administered by the Levitical Priesthood, under which the Hebrew nation lived. These laws were given mostly at Mt. Sinai, with additions, repetitions and explanations, throughout the Wilderness wanderings.

Levites, one tribe out of the Twelve, were set apart for the word of God. God took them, in lieu of first-born sons. God claimed the first-born, both of men and flocks. They were supported by tithes, and had 48 cities (Num. 35:7) - (Josh. 21:19)

One Family of Levities, Aaron and Sons, were set apart to be Priests. The rest of the Levites were to be Assistants to the Priests. Their duties were the care of the Tabernacle, and later, the care of the Temple, and to be Teachers, Scribes, Musicians,

Officers, and Judges. (See 1 Chron.23). Ref. Halley's Bible Handbook, page 134-135.

Aaron and his sons were consecrated to the Priesthood. Previous to the time of Moses, sacrifices were offered by heads of families. But now, the nation was organized and a place set apart for sacrifices, a ritual was prescribed, a special Hereditary order of men was created, in solemn ceremony, for the service. Aaron, and his first-born sons in succession, were High Priests. The priesthood was maintained by the tithes of Levites, and parts of some sacrifice. Here is how they were maintained by tithes, in Num. 18:20-28. Ref. Halley's Bible Handbook, page 135.

The Levitical Priesthood was divinely ordained as mediator between God and the Hebrew nation in the ministry of Animal Sacrifices. These sacrifices were fulfilled in Christ. Animal sacrifices are no longer necessary. Christ Himself is the Great High Priest for Man; the Only Mediator between God and Man. Heb. 8:9-10 - makes this very clear. Ref. Halley's Bible Handbook, page 135.

Levites, the third sons of Jacob and Leah (29:34), ancestors of the tribe of Levites, who were charged with the care of the Tabernacle and the Temple (Num. 8-11). Aaron shall offer the Levites before the Lord for an offering of the children of Israel that they may execute the service of the Lord. Num. 8 "And after that went the Levites in to do their service in the Tabernacle of the congregation before Aaron, and before his sons, as the Lord had commanded Moses concerning the Levites, so did they unto them."

Ref. Smith Bible Dic., page 359 - The Levitical priests served the pattern and type. The ordinances of outward purification signified the true inner cleansing of the heart and conscience from dead works to serve the living God..

Ref. Smith Bible Dic., page 358 - The tribe stood forth separate and apart, recognizing even in this stern work the spiritual as higher than the natural. The tribe of Levi were to take the place of the earlier priesthood of the first-born as representatives of the holiness of the people.

Ref. Smith Bible Dic., page 532 - The idea of a priesthood connects itself in all its forms, pure or corrupted, with the consciousness, more or less distinct, of the sin men feel when they have broken a law. The power above them is holier than they are, and they dare not approach it. They crave for the intervention of someone more likely to be acceptable than themselves. He, the priest, must offer up their prayers, thanksgivings, sacrifice, offerings. He, the Priest, becomes their representative in things pertaining unto God. He may become also, though this does not always follow, the representative of God to man.

Ref. Halley's Bible Dic., page 104 - This polygamous family, with many shameful things to their credit, was accepted of God, as a whole, to be the beginning of the Twelve Tribes which became the Messianic Nation, chosen of God to bring the Savior into the world. This shows:

1. That God uses human beings as they are, to serve His purposes, and, so to speak, does the best He can with the material He has.

2. It is no indication that every one that God thus uses will be eternally saved, only those that serve Him and are true to His word, as He said to You, Pastor. That has changed My holy inspired word for the love of money. When I said if you ask anything in My name, My Father will give it to you, don't suppress My word for filthy-lucre because I said in My holy word in 2Tim. 3:16 "All scri-p ture is inspired by Me-God and is profitable for teaching for reproof, for correction, for training in righteousness. As I said in Heb. 4:12 "For the word of God is living and active and sharper than any two-edged sword, and piering as far as division of soul and spirit, of both joints and

marrow, and able to judge the thoughts and intentions of the heart." One may be useful in serving God's plans in this world, and yet fail to qualify for the eternal world, in that day when God shall judge the secrets of men's hearts for final disposition (Rom. 2:12-16, Acts 10:42, 1Cor. 15:1).

3. It is a testimony to the Truthfulness of Bible writers. No other book narrates with such utter candor the weaknesse of its heroes, and things so contrary to ideals which it aims to promote. Buy those books I used as my References to find out more about the function of Levis and the Priesthood.

God's word is not a tradition that is handed down or an opinion. His word is the truth. He said, I am not a man that I should lie or speak falsely or utter untruth knowingly, as with intent to deceive. Read Isaiah 40:8 and Matt. 24:35 and Mal. 3:6.

Pastor, do you remember what the book of Psalms says about this? That God's words will always prove true and right, no matter who questions them? (5) Pastor, some say, our breaking faith with God is good, our sins serve a good purpose, for people will notice how good God is when they see how bad we are. Is it fair, then, for Him to punish us when our sins are helping Him? That is the way some people talk, Pastor. (6) God forbid. Then what kind of God would He be, to overlook sin? Pastor, we were Gentiles, a Heathen nation in the world without God. When God gave this commandment in the Law for Levi to collect a tenth from the people, that is from their brethren, their brethren were of the twelve tribes of Israel. God's word is infallible, without a mistake. When God said in Rev. 22:18-19 "And I solemnly declare to everyone who reads this book; If anyone adds anything to what is written here God shall add to him the plagues described in this book. (19) And if anyone subtracts any part of these prophecies, God shall take away his share in the Tree of Life, and in the Holy City just described. But some (Pastor) have added to His Word by saying He said for them to collect tithes and tithes were money. 1John 1:6 says, "if we say that we have fellowship wit Him and yet walk in the darkness, we lie and do not practice the truth." They have turned from God's Word for the love of money, and have no faith in God or His Word. Because God said in His Word that He would supply all your needs, according to His riches in glory by Christ Jesus. And whatsoever you ask the Father in My name, He will give it to you. But (some Pastors) have turned, like it says in Jude 1:11 "woe upon them." For they follow the example of Cain who killed his brother; and, like Balaam, they will do anything for money; and like Korah, they have disobeyed God and will die under His curse. They are doing this, have left the truth of God's infallible word and have turned to their own righteousness by turning God's word into a fable. Some Pastors have forgotten that God's word is infallible and trustworthy. Some Pastors have no regard for the truth about His infallible word on tithes. All Pastors know who God called to collect tithes. They that are collecting tithes have no reverence for the truth about God's word, causing us to believe that tithes were money, and God called them to collect tithes, which is false. Have our Pastors transgressed the word of God, by turning away from the truth about His word on tithes. Or have some Pastors, blithely followed their own misguided ideas on doctrine, following the tradition of men.

Mal. 4:4 "Remember the law of Moses My servant, even the statutes and ordinances which I commanded him in Horeb for all Israel." Lev. 27:34 "These are the commandments which the Lord commanded Moses for the sons of Israel at Mount Sinai."

When Preachers or Pastors are teaching their members that tithes are for us today, and that tithes were money, this is so false and deceptive. God said if any man teach otherwise, and consent not to wholesome words, even the words of our Lord Jesus Christ, and the doctrine which is according to godliness, he is proud, knowing nothing, but doting about questions and strifes of words, whereof cometh envy, strife, railings, evil surmisings. When a Pastor turns God's word into a fable, you don't know God, you are deceiving yourself, because God said, in 2John 1:9 "Whosoever transgresseth and abideth not in the doctrine of Christ, hath not God, He that abideth in the doctrine of Christ, he hath both the Father and the Son." God said in 1Pet. 5:3 "neither as being lords over God's heritage, but being examples to the flock. But you have, Pastor, become over God's flock, by changing His word about tithes, by deceiving your members in deluding the truth about God's word, misleading and deceiving yourself about tithes.

Most all churches use this scripture in Mal. 3:10 "Bring the whole tithes into the storehouse, so that there may be food in My house, and test Me now in this, says the Lord of Hosts. If I will not open for you the windows of heaven, and pour you out a blessing until it overflows."

God never said in His holy inspired infallible word that tithes were money when He said bring in the tithes, so that there would be food in My house. He was not speaking to us about bringing Him money so there would be food in His house. He was not speaking to us, but speaking to the Israelites of the nation of Israel, because the Church is not a storehouse. The Church is the Body of Christ, not a storehouse. We that are Christians are members of that Church, which is Christ's body. The storehouse is where the nation of Israel brought the tithes, which was food, 2 Chron. 31:5 "And as soon as the order spread, the sons of Israel provided in abundance the first fruits of grain, new wine, oil, honey and all the produce of the field; and they brought in abundantly the tithes of all." (6) Here is what God is saying, bring food into the storehouse. In this book, I have explained sacred gifts and consecrated things were the first-born animals. Deu. 26:12 "When you have finished paying all the tithe of your increase in the third year, the year of tithing, then you shall give it to the Levite, to the stranger, to the orphan and to the widow, that they may eat in your towns, and be satisfied." Now you see what tithes were, God said bring into My storehouse so that there will be food in My house. Neh:13-12, Neh: 35-39

Here are some Scriptures where God is talking about false teachers. 2Tim. 3:8 "And these teachers fight truth just as Jannes and Jambres fought against Moses. They have dirty minds, and have turned against Christian faith." Some Pastors are not accepting God's word in faith and confidence with spiritual acceptance of truth or realities not certified by reason, believing in God's word. They don't have faith that God said in His word. He would supply all their needs according to His riches in glory by Christ Jesus. God said without faith it is impossible to please Him, for he who comes to God must believe that he is a rewarder of those who seek Him. Some Pastors have lost faith in what God said, by turning tithes into money. Some Pastors don't have trust in what He said tithes were. But many church Pastors have turned from this truth to teach a fable about tithes being money. We, as God's children, we believe in God's word by faith and spiritual acceptance, but our faith can be taken from us if we put our faith in some Pastor's saying, because faith is trusting in God's word with spiritual acceptance, not in what a Pastor says. God said My word is true, because there will be false teachers. This is why we should study the scripture by putting our faith in what a Pastor says about tithes, then our faith is not in God's word. Then, there is nothing God can do, until we put our faith in Him, and in His word, because He created us and gave us a free will. We can believe in what His word says about tithes by our faith, and spiritual acceptance, by faith in,

God's word.

2Tim. 3:8 "And these teachers fight truth just as Jannes and Jambres fought against Moses."

2Tim. 3:13 "In fact, evil men and false teachers will become worse and worse, deceiving many, they themselves have been deceived by Satan."

An evil and false teacher is one who is morally wrong, as some Pastors are who are teaching tithes mean money. This is what God is saying about anyone who is teaching His word falsely, about tithes being money. They know what is true, but change My word for the love of money. I said I would supply all your needs, Pastor, you don't have to change My word to get what you need, because I said whatsoever you ask the Father in My name, He will give it to you. Some of you Pastors don't have any faith in My inspired infallible Word, and it is impossible to please Me without faith.

Titus 1:16 "They profess to know God, but by their deeds they deny Him, being detestable and disobedient, and worthless for any good deeds."

2 Tim. 3:9 - But they won't get away with all this forever. Some day their deceit will be well known to every one, as was the sin of Jannes and Jambres.

Col 2:8 "See to it that no one take you captive through philosophy and empty deception, according to the tradition of men, according to the elementary principles of the World, rather than according to Christ."

Col. 2:8 "Don't let others spoil your faith and joy with their philosophies, their wrong and shallow answers built on men's thoughts and ideas, instead of what Christ has said."

Col. 2:8 "Beware lest any man spoil you through philosophy and vain deceit. After the tradition of men, after the rudiments of the world, and not after Christ."

2 John 1:9 "Whosoever transgresseth, and abideth not

in the doctrine of Christ, hath not God. He that abideth in the doctrine of Christ, he hath both the Father and the Son."

2 John 1:9 "Anyone who goes too far and does not abide in the teaching of Christ, does not have God; the one who abides in the teaching, he has both the Father and the son."

2 John 1:9 "For if you wander beyond the teaching of Christ, you will leave God behind, while if you are loyal to Christ's teachings, you will have God too. Then you will have both the Father and the Son."

1 John 2:16 "For all these worldly things, these evil desires, the craze for sex, the ambition to buy everything that appeals to you and the pride that comes from wealth and importance — these are not from God. They are from this evil world itself."

1 John 2:16 "For all that is in the world, the lust of the flesh and the lust of eyes and the boastful pride of life, is not from the Father, but is from the World."

1 John 2:17 "And the world is passing away, and also its lusts; but the will of God abides forever."

God is saying in 1 John 2:16 - that all in the world is evil desire and the lust of the flesh, and the boastful pride of life that comes from wealth.

This is what some Pastors are doing when they change tithes to money, they are craving for the love of money, by their desire.

1 John 2:17 - God is saying this to all. "And the World is passing away, and so it's lust. The unlawful lust for money has caused some pastors to change what tithes are.

1 John 1:6 "If we say that we have fellowship with Him, and walk in darkness, [Pastor] we lie and do not speak the truth."

1 John 2:6 "He that saith he abideth in Him ought himself also, so to walk, even as He walked." (Pastor)

1 John 2:15 "Love not the World or money, neither the things that are in the World, Pastor, if any man love the World's money, the love of the Father is not in him."

1 John 5:17 - God is saying in 2 John 1:9 - Transgressing His word means to break or violate to sin. 1 John 5:17 says all unrighteousness is sin. When a Pastor asks for tithes this is unrighteousness, and all unrighteousness is sin, if you don't know, Pastor.

3 John 1:11 "Beloved, follow not that which is evil, but that which is good. He that doeth good is of God; but he that doeth evil hath not seen God."

1 John 1:6 God says if we have fellowship with Him we don't walk in darkness, and don't lie, but tell the truth about His word on tithes.

Rom. 2:21 "Thou therefore which teachest another, teachest thou not thy self? Thou that preachest a man should not steal, dost thou steal?"

Rom. 2:21 "Yes, you teach others - then why don't you teach yourselves? You tell others not to steal - do you steal - do you steal?"

Rom. 2:21 "You, therefore, who teach another, do you not teach yourself? You who preach that one should not steal, do you steal?"

Rom. 2:21 - God is saying in this Scripture, to all Pastors that are collecting tithes falsely, and saying tithes are money. You are stealing in My Holy name by taking tithes, by lying about tithes being money? Thou therefore (Pastor) which teachest another, teachest thou not thyself? Thou that preachest a man should not steal, dost thou steal, means you steal in My name by lying about what I said. I called only the Levi in Heb. 7:5 - and tithes are not money. You, as Pastor, you are stealing by your taking tithes, by dishonestly saying it is money. Ask your Pastor, "Are you being dishonest or wrong by stealing in God's name, by collecting tithes and saying tithes were money. This is stealing, Pastor, knowing that tithes were not for us and not money. Pastor, nothing is done secretly, because Heb. 4:12 says "The word of God is living and active and sharper than any two-edged sword and piercing, as far as division of soul and spirit, of both joints and marrow, and able to judge the thoughts and intentions of heart." God said that no one will get away with anything. His spirit judges the thoughts and intentions of our hearts. God knows why some Pastors take tithes, for the love of money. But God knows deep into our innermost thoughts and desires, with all their parts, exposing us for what we really are, Pastor, and His word discerns the thoughts and intents of your heart, why some Pastors are lying about tithes being money.

Rom. 2:22 "Thou that sayest a man should not commit adultery, dost thou commit adultery? Thou that abhorrest idols, dost thou commit sacrilege?"

Rom. 2:22 "You say it is wrong to commit adultery - do you do it? You say, Don't pray to idols, and then make money your god instead."

Rom. 2:22 "You who say that one should not commit adultery, do you commit adultery? You who abhor idols, do you rob temples?"

Rom. 2:22 - God is saying in this Scripture some people make money by lying about God's word about tithes being money. Some pastors are stealing money by lying about tithes. Anything taken dishonestly, without our acknowledgment is stealing.

"But the young man heard that saying, he went away sorrowful; for he had great possessions." He didn't steal, but all the time money was his God, as some Pastors are doing, stealing money secretly, and dishonestly.

Rom. 6:16 "Don't you realize that you can choose your own master? You can choose a sin [with death] or else obedience [with acquittal]. The one to whom you offer yourself he will take you and be your master and you will be his slaves."

Rom 6:16 "Know ye not, that to whom ye yield yourselves servants to obey, his servants ye are to whom ye obey; whether of sin unto death, or of obedience unto righteousness."

Rom. 6:16 "Do you not know that when you present yourselves to someone as slaves for obedience, you are slaves of the one whom you obey, either of sin resulting in death, or of obedience resulting in righteousness."

God is saying in Rom 6:16 - To all of us, Pastor, you can choose. You can choose sin.

God is saying in Rom 6:16 that His word is the truth, on what it says about tithes, but you can choose who is your Master — the Lord or the god of this world? Who do you believe, the word of God, or the god of this world? Or you can choose sin. All sin is unrighteousness, or you can be obedient to His word. God is asking who is your master or who do you serve? The one you are serving is your master.

Acts 20:28 "And now beware: Be sure that you feed and shepherd God's flock, His Church, purchased with His Blood - for the Holy Spirit is holding you responsible as overseers."

God is saying in Acts 20:28 to all, Pastor, to beware, don't deceive My Church by misleading them and saying tithes are money. God is saying to be prudent. God is saying to all Pastors to shepherd His flock. God is saying that the Holy Spirit is holding you responsible as overseers.

Isaiah 40:8 says His word stands forever on what He says about tithes. It cannot be changed by no man. Jesus said His word stands forever.

Some Pastors have no faith in what God's word says about tithes. They have left God's word, by not feeding or shepherding His flock. The Holy Spirit is holding you, Pastor, responsible for this unrighteousness about tithes. For the love of money, which is the roof of all evil, Pastor, which some Pastors have coveted after, you have erred from your faith in God's word, Pastor, and pierced yourself through many sorrows. Some Pastors have even turned away from God's word, because of their love for money by not believing that God's word says tithes are not money. But, some Pastors have tried to change what His word says. But God says in His word that His word is the truth and let every man be a liar.

1 Tim. 6:5 "These arguers, their minds warped by sin, don't know how to tell the truth; to them the Good News is just a means of making money. Keep away from them.

1 Tim. 6:5 - God says, Here is what I am saying tithes were in 2 Chron. 31:5-6; Deu. 26:12; Num. 18:24-28; Deu. 14:22 - this is the law of tithes. Some Pastors are favoring a proposition or disputation, a plan to scheme us by saying tithes are money. Every man is a liar. My word is true.

1 Tim. 6:5 - God is saying, some Pastors are turning aside from His word about what tithes are. Some Pastors have turned to error and are corrupt. This is what God is saying, they argue their minds in sin, they are using false judgment by misleading us about tithes being money. This is what God is saying in this Scripture, that the Pastor, with his mind warped in sin, has distorted the truth about tithes. This is what God is saying about anyone that sins. Pastor, you are sinning by changing God's word to a fable about tithes being money. This is wrong, wickedness, injustice. God said what tithes are. His word is the truth and let every man be a liar about what tithes were. God is not a man that He should lie about tithes.

God is saying in 1 Tim. "Perverse disputings of men of corrupt minds, and destitute of the truth, supposing that gain is godliness; from such withdraw thyself." 1 Tim. 6:5 "And constant friction between men of depraved minds and deprived of the truth, who suppose that godliness is a means of gain."

95

God is saying in 2 Tim. 3:8 "And these teachers fight truth just as Jannes and Jambres fought against Moses. They have dirty minds, warped and twisted, and have turned against the Christian faith."

God is saying in Titus 1:11 "Whose mouths must be stopped, who subvert whole houses, teaching things which they ought not, for filthy lucre's sake."

God is saying in 1 Tim 6:7 "For we brought nothing into this world, and it is certain we can carry nothing out."

God is saying in 2 Tim 3:9 "But they won't get away with all this forever. Some day their deceit will be known to every one, as was the sin of Jannes and Jambres."

God said in 2 Tim 4:4 "They won't listen to what the Bible says but will blithely follow their own misguided ideas."

2 Tim. 4:4 - God is saying in this scripture, that they won't listen in order to hear what the Bible says, the sacred writing of the Christian religion, but will blithely follow their own misguided ideas, swayed by joy of the moment without thought of the future.

Our Pastors are teaching that tithes are money. God is saying in Rom. 3:4 - Of course not. Though everyone else in the world is a liar, God is not. Do you remember what the book of Psalms says about this? That God's words will always prove true and right, no matter who questions them.

Rom. 3:4 - God is saying in this scripture to us all, and also to all Pastors that are teaching that tithes are money to their members, that tithes have never been money, and everyone else (Pastor) in the world is a liar, that teaches tithes were money.

Rom. 3:4 "May it never be; Rather, let God be found true, though every man be found a liar, as it is Written. That Thou mightest be justified in thy words. And mightest prevail when Thou art judged."

Psalms 116:11 "I said in my haste. All men are liars."

Psalms 51:4 "Against thee, thee only, have I sinned, and done this evil in thy sight; that thou mightest be justified when thou speakest, and be clear when thou judgest."

Rom. 3:5 "But, some say our breaking faith with God is good, our sins serve a good purpose, for people will notice how good God is when they see how bad we are. Is it fair, then, for Him to punish us when our sins are helping Him?"

Rom. 3:5 "But if our unrighteousness commend the righteousness of God, what shall we say? Is God unrighteous who takes vengeance?"

Rom. 3:5 - God is saying in this scripture, is God unrighteous who taketh vengeance? Is this you, Pastor, when you are taking tithes?

Rom. 3:6 - "God forbid! Then what kind of God would He be, to overlook sin? How could He ever condemn anyone?"

Rom. 3:7 "But if through my lie the truth of God abounded to His glory, why am I also still being judged as a sinner?"

Rom. 9:19 "You will say to me then, why does He still find fault? For who resists His will?"

Rom. 3:6 - God is saying in this scripture, to all Christians, and to you, also, Pastor, all sin is unrighteousness. Pastor, it is a sin and unrighteous for you as God's shepherd, to change what His word says what tithes are.

Psalm 14:3 "But no, all have strayed away, all are rotten with sin. Not one is good, not one."

God is saying in Psalms 14:3 - To all Christians and also to you, Pastor, who have strayed away from His word and have turned tithes to money, and are teaching tithes in His church today, He said in Heb. 7:5 - who He called to take tithes. Not you, Pastor. He didn't call you. Go back in the scripture and see for yourself who He called to take tithes. He never called any Pastor to take tithes. Tithes were under the law that went out in Rom. 10:4 - Christ is the end of the law, Heb. 8:13. A new covenant hath made the first old. Now that which decayeth and waxeth old is ready to vanish away.

God is saying in Psalm 14:3 - To you, Pastor, that you have strayed away from His word about what tithes are and have tried to change His word on tithes to money. You are rotten with sin. Not one is good, no, not one. But your sins will find you out. Your sins cannot be hidden from God.

1 Thess. 5:22 "Abstain from all appearance of evil."

Col 3:9 "Do not lie to one another, since you laid aside the old self with its evil practice."

God is saying in Col. 3:9 - to all that are Christians, and also to you, Pastor, not to lie about what tithes are not. Rom. 3:4 - That everyone in the world is a liar, God is not, that His word will always prove true and right no matter who questions it.

Col 3:1 "If ye then be risen with Christ, seek those things which are above, where Christ sitteth on the right hand of God."

Psalm 110:1 "The Lord says sit at My right hand, until I make thine enemies a footstool for thy feet.

3 John 1:11 "Beloved, follow not that which is evil, but that which is good. He that doeth good is of God, but he that doeth evil hath not seen God."

God is saying in 3 John 1:11 - to his flock and also to His shepherd over His Church, don't let this bad example influence you. Remember that those who do what is right prove that they are God's children. Pastor, it is showing evil on your part when you change what God's word says about what tithes are. God is saying to His Shepherd it is evil. "Follow not after that, do good, then you will prove that you are My shepherd."

1 John 3:4 "But those who keep on sinning are against God, for every sin is done against the will of God."

1 John 3:5 "And ye know that He was manifested to take away our sin, and in Him is no sin."

1 John 3:6 "So if we stay close to Him, obedient to Him, we won't be sinning either, but as for those who keep on sinning, they should realize this, Pastor, they sin because they have never really known Him or become His.

1 John 3:7 - Little children, let no one deceive you, the one (Pastor) who practices righteousness is righteous, just as He is righteous. Practicing tithes, Pastor, is unrighteousness.

1 John 3:8 "He that committeth sin is of the devil, for the devil sinneth from the beginning. For this purpose the Son of God was manifested, that He might destroy the works of the devil."

1 John 3:8 "But if you keep on sinning, it shows that you belong to Satan, who since he first began to sin has kept steadily at it. But the Son of God came to destroy these works of the devil."

1 John 3:9 "The person who has been born into God's family does not make a practice of sinning, because now God's life is in him, so he can't keep on sinning, for this new life has been born into him and controls him - he has been born again."

God is saying in 1 John 3:6 - To all His flock, also to you, Pastor, that are taking tithes in His Church, and lying about His Word about tithes being money that if we stay close to Him, obedient to Him, we won't be sinning either, but as for those who keep on sinning, they should realize this, they sin because they have never really known Him or become His. God said whosoever is abideth in Him we sinneth not.

God is saying in 1 John 3:6 - Whosoever sinneth hath not seen Him, neither known Him.

1 John 3:8 - God is saying, "he that committeth sin is of the devil - for he sinneth from the beginning. For this purpose the Son of God was manifested, that He might destroy the works of the devil."

1 John 3:9 "No one who is born of God practices sin,

because His seed abides in Him and he cannot sin, because he is born of God."

(Danger of False Teachers)

2 Peter 2:1 - God is talking in this scripture about false teachers. A false teacher is like Pastors who are deceitful and are teaching tithes in His Church today. God said in this scripture, Pastors, that you are a false teacher, teaching tithes is false for us. This is what some Pastors are doing by teaching today contrary to what is true and correct, about who God called to take tithes and what tithes are, by taking tithes and saying tithes are money. Pastor, God never said anything like that. He did say let every man be a liar, but My word is true.

2 Peter 2:3 - This is what God about false teachers. Anyone who is teaching against His word is a false teacher. These teachers in their greed will tell you anything to get hold on your money. They, the Pastors, are teaching tithes for the love of money. But God said in this scripture, he has condemned them long ago and their destruction is on the way.

(Destruction of False Teachers)

2 Peter 2:4 "For if God did not spare angels when they sinned, but cast them into hell and committed them to pits of darkness, reserved for judgment.

1 Peter 4:17 "For the time is come that judgment must begin at the house of God; and if it first begin at us, what shall the end be of them that obey not the gospel of God."·

(The Characteristics of the Godless)

Psalms 14:3 - Pastor, God is saying this about you for taking tithes and saying tithes are money, and tithes are for us today. "They are all gone aside, they are all together become filthy; there is none that doeth good, no not one."

Psalms 14:3 "They all turned aside, together they have become corrupt. There is no one who does good, not even one." 2-2 From the New Open Bible.

Psalms 14:3 "But no, all have strayed away, all are rotten with sin. Not one is good, not one." (1) and (3) came from King James Version and the Living Bible.

God is saying in Psalms 14:3 - That all that have strayed away are rotten with sin.

God is saying that all Pastors that are teaching tithes have strayed away from His word.

(Wicked Judges Will Be Judged)

Psalms 58:3 "The wicked are estranged from the Womb. These who speak lies go astray from birth."

Psalms 52:3 "Thou lovest evil more than good, and lying rather than to speak righteousness."

God is saying in Psalms 52:3 it is evil to lie about Him, Pastor, to say He, God, said for you to take tithes and that tithes are money, and to say He said for us today to bring all the tithes into the storehouse in Mal. 3:10. They are using this scripture in error. The church is not the storehouse, it is the body of Christ.

Psalms 34:14 "Depart from evil, and do good; seek peace and pursue it."

Psalms 34:13 "Keep your tongue from evil, and your lips from speaking deceit." ⸔

(Confession and Forgiveness of Sin)

Psalms 51:1 "Have mercy upon me, O God, according to thy loving kindness, according unto the multitude of they tender mercies blot out my transgression."

WHAT TITHING IS NOT – WHAT NATION IS HE SPEAKING TO

Chapter 9

More scriptures on tithes

R ef. Bible, Dic. page, 242 – On what tithes are. This is what tithes are – they are not money. Tithes are one-tenth. One tenth of all produce of land and herds were set apart under the Levitical law, for the support of the Levites, and a tenth of that went to the priests. There were tithe regulations among other nations. Gen. 14:20, Lev. 27:30,33, Num.18:21-32, Deu.12:17-18, Deu. 14:22-28. The Pharisees tithed their mint, anise-cummin and rue. Matt. 23:23 is a scripture churches use in error with the intent to mislead and cheat us. Pastors say, 'see in Matt. 23:23, Jesus was teaching tithing to the Pharisees.' But tithes were not money. Jesus was speaking of their tithes of mint, dill, cummin and rue. These things came from their produce – what they sowed. These were things which came from the field each year. Here is where the Pharisees tithes came from – Deu. 14:22. What they tithed was what came from the field — everything which they sowed. Tithes are not money as Pastors are teaching falsely, to deceive us and to defraud us. God said let every man be a lie about tithes, but He is not a man to lie, and His word will prove true.

First Fruits – God claimed as His own. Not only the tithes, but the first-born sons of all families (in lieu of whom he accepted the tribe of Levi), and first-born of all flocks and herds and first fruits of the field. The first fruits of the harvest were to be offered at Passover, and no part of the new crop of a young orchard (the 4th year) was to be given to God, and no fruit of it could be used until this was done. The lesson is to make God first in life.

Now you have read what the Bible Dic. and the Halley's Bible Handbook says about what tithing was and what it was used for. Now I will show you some scriptures on Spoils. Abram gave Melchizedek spoils after his victory. The spoils he gave him were not money.

Heb. 7:4 "Now observe how great this man was [Melchizedek] to whom Abraham, the patriarch, gave a tenth of the choicest spoils." Now when you read, Gen. 14:11-24, you will see that Abram went to war, won the victory, brought back all the goods. Gen. 14:20 says Abram gave him [Melchizedek] a tenth of all. (16) says goods are wholesome, as meat, or fruit. (24) "Abram said I will take nothing, except what the men have eaten." Heb.7:1-2 - When Abraham was returning home after winning a great battle against many Kings, Melchizedek met him and blessed him. The Abraham took a tenth of all goods he had won in the battle and gave it to Melchizedek. Heb. 7:4 - Even Abraham, the first and most honored of all God's chosen people, gave Melchizedek a tenth of the spoils he took from the kings he had been fighting. But most all churches use Gen. 14:20 to say, see, Abraham gave Melchizedek a tithe and it was a tenth. They use that scripture in error, falsely to mislead us from the truth, for one purpose, that is to cheat us. The Pastors know what Abram gave Melchizedek, and it was not money, it was spoils. Gen. 14:20 - King James Version and the Living Bible says, "Then Abram gave Melchizedek a tenth of all the loot, the spoils and loot Abram took from war and God gave him Mechizedek a tenth of all spoils, goods, and loot." It wasn't money he gave him, but your Pastor wants you to believe it was money. (Read Gen. 14:11-24 to get a better understanding of what he gave to. Melchizedek. (King James Version and the Living Bible. Also read Heb. 7:1-2) ~

Remember that God's word is infallible, there are no mistakes in His word. It is exempt from liability to error, or moral failure, absolutely trustworthy and sure, not liable to error.

Jesus said that His word, the word of God, is true and you shall know the truth and the truth shall make you free from the burden of unresolved guilt. His word is the only truth, God is true to His word. His word is the same yesterday, today, and forever. His word lasts throughout eternity.

(Scripture on the Law of Tithes)

Deu. 14:22 "This scripture is the law on tithing. You shall surely tithe all the produce from what you sow, which comes out of the field every year."

The churches are teaching God's flock that tithes are money, but the scripture says differently. Who do you believe, God's Inspired Infallible word, or your Pastor?

God said in Deu. 14:22 - Living bible and King James Version, "Thou shalt truly tithe all the increase of they seed, that the field bringeth forth year by year." This is what the Bible says tithes are, but our Pastors don't believe this. They are using their own misguided ideas about what tithes should be. (22) You must tithe all of your crops every year. The Bible says what tithes are and to tithe once a year, but Pastors say to tithe each week. How can this be so, when God's Inspired Infallible word without error says differently. No Pastor has the right to change what God's word says about tithes. God said tithes are paid once a year, and that tithes are not money. How can our Church Pastor say that tithing is money and that we should pay our tithes each week, when the scriptures say differently?

How can any Pastor change God's inspired infallible word?

✝ Deu. 14:23 - Law of the tithes. This is the one thing tithes are for (23) "And you shall eat in the presence of the Lord your God, where He chooses to establish His name, the tithe of your grain, your new wine, your oil, and the first born of your herd and your flock, in order that you may learn to fear the Lord your God always." Now that you have read Chapter 14:23, about what tithes were, you know some Pastors are teaching this false doctrine on tithes.

⚹ The Living Bible, Deu. 14:22-23 "You must tithe all of your crops every year." (23) "Bring the tithe to eat before the Lord your God at the place he shall choose as His sanctuary; this applies to your tithes of grain, new wine, olive oil, and the first-born of your flocks, and herds. The purpose of tithing is to teach you always to put God first in your lives."

Lev. 27:30 - Living Bible "A tenth of the produce of the land, whether grain or fruit, is the Lord's and is holy." (32) "And the Lord owns every tenth animal of your herds and flocks and other domestic animals, as they pass by for counting."

Deu. 14:24 "And if the distance is so great for you that you are not able to bring the tithe, since the place where the Lord your God chooses to set His name is too far away from you, when the Lord your God blesses you."

It is deception, and evil morally wrong, immoral of you, Pastor, to deceive us about tithes being money. God is saying in Deu. 14:25 "Then you shall exchange it for money, and bind the money in your hand and go to the place which the Lord your God chooses." (25) How can tithes be money, as churches are teaching? If tithes were money, why would God say this in Deu. 14:25?

Deu. 14:26 - this is what God said to do with the money,

after selling your tithes. "When you arrive, use the money to buy an ox, a sheep, some wine, or beer, to feast there before the Lord your God, and to rejoice with your household. Spend the money for whatever your heart desires, for oxen, or sheep, or wine, or strong drink, or whatever your heart desires; and there you shall eat in the presence of the Lord your God and rejoice, you and your household. And thou shalt bestow that money for whatsoever thy soul lusteth after." If tithes were money, God wouldn't say to them to sell their money for money. Why would He?

Deu. 14:27 - God also said to them, "You shall not neglect the Levite who is in your town, for he has no portion or inheritance among you."

Living Bible Deu. 14:27 - King James Version "And the Levite that is within thy gates; Don't forget to share your income with the Levites in your community, for they have no property or crops as you do."

God is saying in Deu. 14:28 - At the end of every third year, you shall bring forth all the tithes of your produce increase in that same year, and shall deposit it up within they gates." Living Bible - Every third year you are to use your entire tithe for local welfare programs. Pastors are teaching tithes for the love of money. Not for righteousness, for filthy lucre.

This is what some of the tithes were used for. Deu. 14:29 "And the Levite because he the Levite hath no part nor inheritance with thee, and the stranger and the fatherless, and the widow, which are within thy gates, shall come, and shall eat and be satisfied; that the Lord thy God may bless thee in all the work of thine hand which thou doest.

Deu. 12:17 "Thou mayest not be allowed to eat within your gates the tithe of your grain, or new wine, or oil, or the first-born of your herd or flock, or any of your votive offerings which you vow, or your freewill offerings, or the contribution of your hand."

God is saying in Deu. 12:17 - These tithes, or grain, or

oil, or new wine were holy to the Lord, as I said in Lev. 27:30 - all the tithes of the land, of the seed of the land, or of the fruit of the tree is the Lord's; it is holy to the Lord.

A vow is a solemn promise made to God to perform or to abstain from performing a certain thing. Vows were entirely voluntary, but once made were regarded as compulsory votive offerings arising from the produce of any impure traffic were wholly forbidden. Freewill is a voluntary offering.

Deu. 26:12 "When you have finished paying all the tithes of your increase in the third year, the year of tithing, then you shall give it to the Levite, to the stranger, to the orphan and to the widow, that they may eat in your towns, and be satisfied." Living Bible - "Every third year is a year of special tithing. That year you are to give all your tithes to the Levites, migrants, orphans, and widows, so that they will be well fed. (13) Then you shall declare before the Lord your God, I have given all of my tithes to the Levites, the migrants, the orphans, and the widows, just as you commanded me; I have not violated or forgotten any of your rules. (14) I have not touched the tithe while I was ceremonially defiled, [for instance, while I was in mourning] nor have I offered any of it tot he dead. I have obeyed the Lord my God and have done everything you commanded me. (15) Look down from your holy home in Heaven and bless your people and the land you have given us, as you promised our ancestors, make it a land flowing with milk and honey." Now you have read the scripture for yourself and found out for yourself, what tithes were, and found out that your Pastor has been teaching a fable.

(The Bible Says Nothing About Tithes Being Money)

Num. 18:20 "Then the Lord said to Aaron, You shall have no inheritance, in their land, nor own any portion among them; I am your portion and your inheritance among the sons of Israel."

Num. 18:20 - Living Bible - "You priests may own no property, nor have any income, for I am all that you need. Thou shall have no inheritance, God said to Aaron. I am your portion, and inheritance."

Num. 18:24 "For the tithes of the sons of Israel, which they offer as an offering to the Lord, I have given to the Levites for an inheritance; therefore I have said concerning them, They shall have no inheritance among the sons of Israel."

Num. 18:25-26 "Then the Lord spoke to Moses, saying, (26) Thus speak unto the Levites, and say unto them, When ye take of the children of Israel the tithes which I have given you from them for your inheritance, ye shall offer up heave offering of it for the Lord, even a tenth part of the tithes."

Num. 18:26 - King James Version, Living Bible "The Lord also said to Moses, Tell Levites to give to the Lord a tenth of the tithes they receive" - a tenth of the tithes to be presented to the Lord by gesture of waving before the altar.

Deu. 26:13 - New International - "Then say to the Lord your God, I have removed from my house the sacred portion, portion and have given it to the Levite, the alien, the fatherless and the widow according to all you commanded. I have not turned aside from your commands nor have I forgotten any of them."

Deu. 26:17 "You have today declared the Lord to be your God, and that you would walk in His ways and keep His ordinances, and listen to His voice." (18) "and the Lord has today declared you to be His people, a treasured possession, as He promised you, and that you should keep all His commandments." (19) "He has declared that He will set you in praise, fame and honor high about all the nations He has made and that you will be a people holy to the Lord your God, as He promised."

Neh. 10:34 "Likewise cast lots for the supply of wood among the priests, the Levites, and the people in order that they might bring it to the house of our God, according to our fathers' households, at fixed times annually, to burn on the altar of the Lord our God as it is written in the law." (Read (33).)

Pharisees cheated widows out of their houses and violently opposed the only completely righteous person who ever lived. Fourteen times in the Gospels hypocrite occurs, nearly always used by our Lord concerning the Pharisees.

Ref. The New Open Bible New American Standard, page 1111 - The word Pharisee means "separated." Their burning desire was to separate themselves from those people who did not observe the laws of tithing and ritual purity - matters they considered very important.

Same, Ref. page 1111 - The Pharisees exerted strong influence in Jesus' time. They supported the scribes and rabbis in their interpretation of the Jewish law as handed down from the time of Moses. In Jesus' day, this interpretation of the law had become more authoritative and binding the law itself. Jesus often challenged these traditional interpretations and the minute rules that had been issued to guide the people in every area of their behavior.

Same Ref. page 1111 - Jesus was also sensitive to the needs and hurts of individuals - an attitude that brought Him into conflict with the Pharisees. Matthew's gospel (23:1-36) contains Jesus' harsh words against the Pharisees. He believed they placed too much emphasis on minor details, while ignoring "the weightier provisions of the law," such as justice and mercy and faithfulness (Matt. 23:23). The Churches are using Matt. 23:23 to support their teachings to collect tithes. Matt. 23:23 doesn't say for us to give tithes or that tithes were money. Deu. 14:22 - says what ever you sow which comes out of the field, is tithes, not money. What comes out of the field is mints, and dill, and cummin, first fruits, and grain, new wine, oil, honey. Jesus was speaking about these as tithes in Matt. 23:23. (Read Luke 11:42)

Lev. 27:31 - New American Standard, This scripture says if you wish to redeem part of His tithes, he shall add to it one-fifth. (Means one-fifth of tithes) if he wishes to redeem part of His tithes.

These scriptures are being used by churches today, saying it means for us to pay our tithes as a tenth of our income (our money). But the scriptures in Bible don't support any church teaching on this. If tithes were money, why would the scriptures say, "if you wish to redeem part of your tithes?" How can any one redeem part of their tithes? If it was money, then add one-fifth to your tithes. This would be so confusing if tithes were money and you wished to redeem part.

In Num. 27:1-11, tithes were given as an inheritance to the Levites. Why don't churches do the same with tithes? Give the tithes as an inheritance. When a Levites Priest died, who inherited the tithes? His tithes, which were given to him as an inheritance, went to a relative, father or daughter, or brother, if he had no sons. The church today doesn't do as the scripture says. Why not?

They use this scripture, in some churches, to support paying tithes. Gen. 28:22 "And this stone, which I have set up as a pillar, will be God's house, and of all that Thou dost give me I will surely give a tenth to Thee."

This scripture, Gen. 28:22, when you cross-reference, sends you to Deu. 14:22 about what Jacob said he would give God. Deu. 14:22 says, "You shall surely tithe all the produce from what you sow, which comes out of your field every year." This is the tenth Jacob gave to God.

Lev. 27:30, "Thus all the tithe of the land, of the seed of the land, or of the fruit of the tree, is the Lord's, it is holy to the Lord." Cross reference sends you to these scriptures.

Chapter 10

About the nation of Israel. Leviticus, the guide book of His redeemed people. What His newly redeemed people did in their apostasy to stop obeying God's ordinances, Laws, and His statutes that governed their religious lives.

And why they stopped paying tithes

Through the Bible in 55 Minutes - Leviticus, the third book in the Bible, takes its name from the tribe of Levi, descendants of one of Jacob's twelve sons. This tribe had been chosen by God to have charge of the sacred things, and from it came the priests. Later when the nation was established, this tribe was responsible for the temple, its service, its music, its offerings, everything that had to do with the temple worship and upkeep.

Through the Bible in 55 Minutes - This book of Leviticus, also written by Moses gives detailed instructions and descriptions of the special offerings that were prescribed for the feasts, ceremonies, and rituals. These offerings and sacrifices pointed forward to Christ, the true sacrifice for sin. They were the shadow cast backward through the centuries by the cross, the shadow of things to come, about which the Apostle Paul spoke in

Colossians 2:17, Heb. 8:5 and 10:1.

Ref. New Open Bible, page 115 - Leviticus is God's guidebook for His newly redeemed people, showing them how to worship, serve and obey a Holy God. Fellowship with through sacrifice, which is an offering, and obedience shows the awesome holiness of the God of Israel. Leviticus focuses on the worship and walk of the nation of God. "You shall be holy for I the Lord your God am holy." Israel was redeemed and established as a Kingdom of priests and a holy nation. God must be approached by the sacrificial offering.

Leviticus centers around the concept of the holiness of God, and how an unholy people can acceptably approach Him and then remain in continued fellowship. The way to God is only through blood sacrifice, and the walk with God is only through obedience to His law.

The Israelites serve a holy God, who requires them to be holy as well, to be holy means to be separated from other nations.

The blood sacrifice reminds the worshiper that because of sin the Holy God requires the costly gift of life. The blood of the innocent sacrificial animal becomes the substitute for the life of the guilty offerer. Without shedding of blood there is no forgiveness. (Heb. 2:22)

Leviticus can also be called the book of the law of the priest, as it contains very little historical matter, concerning itself with priestly legislation and the practice of the law among the people. Importance is placed upon Israel's separation from all heathen influence so that the nation may retain its religious purity.

Here are some things Israel did to stop bringing tithes to God. Ref. Through the Bible in 55 Minutes. Malachi, the name means Messenger - In spite of the return of God's people from captivity to their homeland, their hearts remained in a far country of disobedience and forgetfulness of God's laws and His mercies. Eight times in this short book, God calls attention to different aspects of His people's apostasy. Apostasy is an abandonment of what one has professed.

Here are scriptures to show readers of this book what Israel did in its disobedience to stop bringing God tithes and offerings. God said in Num. 18:26 - to present Him an offering from their tithes, but in Lev. 1:3 - God said His offering should be without defect. In Lev. 3:1 - He says the same things. Lev. 3:1 "His offering should be without defect. They keep the best, and rob God out of the best offerings and keep the best for themselves." Mal. 1:7 "You are presenting defiled food upon My altar. But you say, How have we defiled Thee? In that you say, The table of the Lord is to be despised. (8) But when you present the blind for sacrifice, is it not evil? And when you present the lame and sick, is it not evil? Why not offer it to your governor? Would he be pleased with you? Or would he receive you kindly? says the Lord of Hosts." Mal. 1:6 "A son honors his father, and a servant his master. Then, if I am a father, where is My honor? And if I am a master, where is My respect? says the Lord of Hosts to you, priests who despise My name. But you say, How have we despised Thy name." Read Mal. 1:7-8.

After that nation of Israel stopped obeying God's ordinances, statutes, and covenant. To walk with God is only through obedience to His law.

But they stopped serving God, and went to serve the Philistines's gods (Dagon, Baal, Ashtoreth), and in Lev. 19:4 - God said to them, " Do not turn to idols or make for yourselves Molten gods. I am the Lord your God." Ex. 34:14 "You shall not worship other god." Ex. 23:24 "You shall not worship their gods." Dagon, the Fish-God of the nation of Philistines, Baal - the supreme male divinity of the Phoenician, and Ashtoreth, their supreme female divinity in their disobedience and forgetfulness of God's law, they followed the practice of other nations, ' and they worshipped idols, and turned from God. This is why they stopped paying God tithes and offerings. In Mal. 3:8 - This is why God said you are robbing Me of tithes and offerings.

Malachi is the last book of the Old Testament and belongs to the period of Nehemiah. The prophets' message is to the priests and the people of Israel, charging them with indifference, doubt, and immorality. Malachi tells of the coming day of the Lord and closes the book with a prophecy of John the Baptist.

Malachi, a prophet, in the days of Nehemiah, directs his message of judgment to a people plagued with corrupt priests' wicked practices, and a false sense of security in their privileged relationship with God. Using the question and answer method, Malachi probes deeply into their problems of hypocrisy, infidelity, mixed marriages, divorce, false worship, and arrogance. So sinful has the nation become the God's words to the people no longer have any impact. For four hundred years after Malachi's ringing condemnations, God remains silent. Only with the coming of John the Baptist (3:1) does God again communicate to His people through a prophet's voice.

Although an exact date cannot be established for Malachi, internal evidence can be used to deduce an approximate date. The Persian term for governor, pechah (1:8, Neh. 5:14, Hag. 1:1, 14: 2,21), indicates that this book was written during the Persian domination of Israel (539-333bc). Sacrifices were being offered in the temple (1:7-10, 3:8) which was rebuilt in 516BC. Evidently many years had passed since the offerings were instituted, because the priests had grown tired of them and corruption had crept into the system. In addition, Malachi's oracle was inspired by the same problems that Nehemiah faced; corrupt priests (1:6; 2:9; Neh. 13:1-9), neglect of tithes and offerings (3:7-12; Neh. 13:10-13), and intermarriage with pagan wives (2:10-16; Neh.13:23-28). Nehemiah came to Jerusalem in 444BC, to rebuild the city walls, thirteen years after Ezra's return and reforms (457BC). Nehemiah returned to Persia in 432BC, but came back to Palestine about 425BC, and dealt with the sins described in Malachi. It is therefore likely that Malachi proclaimed his message while Nehemiah was absent between 432BC and 425BC, almost a century after Haggai and Zechariah began to prophesy (520BC)

The word; an appeal to Backsliders - The diving dialogue in Malachi's prophecy is designed as an appeal to break through the barrier of Israel's disbelief, disappointment, and discouragement. The promised time of prosperity has not yet come, and the prevailing attitude that it is not worth serving God becomes evident in their moral and religious corruption. However, God reveals His continuing love in spite of Israel's lethargy. The people and priests must stop and realize that their lack of blessing is not caused by God's lack of concern but by their disobedience of the covenant law. When they repent and return to God with sincere hearts, the obstacles to the flow of divine blessings will be removed, Malachi also reminds the people that a day of reckoning will surely come when God will judge the righteous and the wicked.

The Privilege of the Nation (1:1-5). The Israelites blind themselves to God's love for them. Wallowing in the problems of the present, they are forgetful of God's works for them in the past. God gives them a reminder of His special love by contrasting the fates of Esau (Edom) and Jacob (Israel).

The Pollution of the Nation (1:6 and 3:15); The priests have lost all respect for God's name and in their greed offer only diseased and imperfect animals on the altar. They have more respect for the Persian governor that they do for the living God. God is withholding His blessings from them because of their disobedience to God's covenant and their insincere teaching.

The people are indicted for their treachery in divorcing the wives of their youth in order to marry foreign women (2:10-16). In response to their questioning the justice of God, they receive a promise of the Messiah's coming but also a warning of the judgment that He will bring (2:17 and 3:6). The people have robbed God of the tithes and offerings due Him, but God is ready to bless them with abundance if they will put Him first (3:7-12). The final problem is the arrogant challenge to the character of God (3:13-15), and this challenge is answered in the remainder of the book. ·

The Promises to the Nation (3:16 and 4:6); The Lord assures His people that a time is coming when the wicked will be judged and those who fear Him will be blessed. The day of the Lord will reveal that it is not "vain to serve God." (3:14).

Internally, they wonder whether it is worth serving God after all. Externally these attitudes surface in mechanical obser-vances, empty ritual, cheating on tithes and offerings, and crass indifference to God's moral and ceremonial law. Their priests are corrupt and their practices wicked, but they are so spiritual insen-sitive that they wonder why they are not being blessed by God. ·

Using a prolong series of questions and answers, God seeks to pierce their hearts of stone. In each case the divine accu-sations are denied. How has God loved us? (1:2-5). How have we priest despised God's name? (1:6-29). How have we people profaned the covenant? (2:10-16). How have we wearied God? (2:1-7 and 3:6). How have we robbed God? (3:7-12). How have we spoken against God? (3:13-15) In effect, the people sneer. Oh, come on now, it's not that bad. However, their rebellion is quiet, not open. As their perception of God grows dim, the resulting materialism and externalism become settled charac-teristics that later grip the religious parties of the Pharisees and Sadducees. In spite of all this, God still loves His people and once again extends His grace to any who will humbly turn to Him. Malachi explores the privilege of the nation (1:1-5), the pollu-tion of the nation (1:6 and 3:15), and the promise of the nation (3:16 and 1:16).

Malachi ends on the bitter word "curse." Although the people are finally cursed of idolatry, there is little spiritual progress in Israel's history. Sin abounds, and the need for the coming Messiah is greater than ever.

"Behold, I am going to send My messenger, and he will clear the way before Me. And the Lord, whom you seek, will suddenly come to His temple, and the messenger of the covenant, in whom you delight, behold, He's coming, says the Lord of Hosts." (2:17 and 3:1)

The Mosaic Covenant was added alongside the Abrahamic Covenant so that the people of Israel would know how to conduct their lives until the seed, the Christ comes and makes the complete and perfect sacrifice, offering for sins. To which the sacrifice of the Mosaic Covenant only points. The Mosaic Covenant was never given so that by keeping it people could be saved, but so that might realize that they cannot do what God wants them to do, even when God writes it down on tablets of stone. The law was given that man might realize that he is helpless and hopeless when left to himself, and realize that his only hope is to receive the righteousness of God by faith in Jesus. Under the Mosaic law the sacrifice were animals that the priests offered on an altar for their sins. Only the blood of Jesus can take away our sins. Christ was foreordained as a sacrifice, slain before the foundation of the world.

Here are some scriptures to show you from God's inspired Holy infallible word how the people of Israel stopped giving God His tithes. This is where offerings used as a sacrifice came from, Num. 18:26- Ref. Smith Bible Dic., page 459 - says an offering was a sacrifice that came out of tithes, in Num. 18:26 - that the newly redeemed people were to worship, and serve and obey a Holy God, fellowship with Him through sacrifice and offering, and walk with God only through obedience to His law and to be separate from other nations. In spite of the return of

119

God's people from captivity to their homeland, their hearts remained in the far country of disobedience and forgetfulness of God's law.

Things they did in disobedience to God's laws about giving tithes.

Lev. 22:21 "And when a man offers a sacrifice of peace offerings to the Lord to fulfill a special vow, or for a freewill offering, of the herd or of the flock, it must be perfect to be accepted, there shall be no defect in it." Mal. 1:8 "But when you present the blind for sacrifice, is it not evil? And when you present the lame and sick, it is not evil."

Jere. 11:6 "The Lord said to me, Proclaim all these words in the towns of Judah and in the streets of Jerusalem. Listen to the terms of this Covenant and follow them." Ref. New International Bible.

Jere. 11:7 "From the time I brought your forefathers up from Egypt until today, I warned them again and again, saying, Obey Me." (The Covenant God is referring to is the Mosaic Covenant.)

Jere. 11:8 "Yet they did not obey or incline their ear, but walked, each one, in the stubbornness of his evil heart; therefore I brought on them all the words of this covenant, which I commanded them to do, but they did not."

Jere. 11:9 "Then the Lord said to Me, a conspiracy has been found among the inhabitants of Jerusalem."

Jere. 11:10 - New International Bible, "They have returned to the sins of their forefathers, who refused to listen to My words. They had followed other gods to serve them. Both the house of Israel and the house of Judah have broken the covenant I made with their forefathers."

Jere. 11:10 - They rebelled against God and broke His

covenant not to serve any other gods. But they refused to listen, but went and served other gods. They stopped paying tithes, and offerings, to God. They left God to serve idols.

Jere. 11:11 "This is what the Lord said to them, Behold I am bringing disaster on them which they will not be able to escape; though they will cry to Me, yet I will not listen to them."

Jere. 11:12 "Then they will pray to their idols and burn incense before them, but that cannot save them form their time of anguish and despair."

Jere. 11:13 "You have as many gods as you have towns, O Judah, and the altar you have set up to burn incense to that shameful god Baal are as many as the streets of Jerusalem."

Jere. 11:17 - Open Bible - "It is because of the wickedness of Israel and Judah in offering incense to Baal that the Lord Almighty who planted the tree has ordered it destroyed."

This is why God said He was being robbed of tithes and offerings, because the nation of Israel was called to worship, serve and obey a Holy God, to walk with God is only through obedience to His law.

Judges 10:6 - Israel, sins - Then the sons of Israel again did evil in the sight of the Lord, served the Baals and the Ashtaroth, the gods of Aram, the gods of Sidon, the gods of Moab, the gods of Ammon, and the gods of the Philistines; thus they forsook the Lord and did not serve Him."

Now you have seen why God said in Malachi, "Return unto Me, you are robbing Me." They turn from God to serve and worship idols.

Here are some of the gods the Israelites served, when they turned from serving the living God.

Ref. Smith Bible Dic., page 70. Baal, the supreme male divinity of the Phoenician and Canaanite nations. Ashtoreth was their supreme female divinity. Some suppose Baal to correspond to the sun and Ashtoreth to the moon, others that Baal was

Jupiter and Ashtoreth Venus. There can be no doubt of the very high antiquity of the worship of Baal. It prevailed in the time of Moses among the Moabites and Midianites. Num. 22:41 and through them spread to the Israelites. Num. 25:3-18 and Deu. 4:3. In the times of the Kings it became the religion of the court and people of the ten tribes. 1 Kings 16:31-33 and 18:19-22, and appears never to have permanently abolished among them. 2 Kings 17:16. Temples were erected to Baal in Judah, 1 Kings 16:32, and he was worshipped with much ceremony, 1 Kings 18:19,26,28. 2 Kings 10:22. The attractiveness to the Jews of this worship undoubtedly grew out of its licentious character. We find this worship also in Phoenician colonies. The religion of the ancient British Islands much resembled this ancient worship of Baal, and may have been derived from it. Nor need we hesitate to regard the Babylonian Bel, Isa. 46:1 - or Belus, as essentially identical with Baal, though perhaps under some modified form. The plural Baalim, is found frequently, showing that he was probably worshipped under different compounds.

Here are some scriptures to show how Israel turned from God to idol worship.

Num. 25:1-3 "While Israel remained at Shittim, the people began to play the harlot with the daughters of Moab. They played with good for nothing women who are practicing prostitution." (Harlots)

Num. 25:2 "For they invited the people to the sacrifices of their gods and the people ate and bowed down to their gods and the people ate and bowed down to their gods."

Num. 25:3 "So Israel joined themselves to Baal of Peor, and the Lord was against Israel.

Things Israel did which caused to God to say
"Return unto Me."

Hosea 9:10 "I found Israel like grapes in the wilderness.
I saw your forefathers as the earliest fruit on the fig tree in its first
season. But they came to Baal-Peor and devoted themselves to
shame. And they became as detestable as that which they loved.
Detestable means extremely hateful, abominable.

1 Kings 16:29-32 - sin of Ahab. (29) "Now Ahab the son
of Omri became King over Israel in the thirty-eighth year of Asa
King of Judah, and Ahab the son of Omri reigned over Israel in
Samaria twenty-two years." (30) "And Ahab the son of Omri did
evil in the sight of the Lord more than all were before him." (31)
"And it came about, as though it had been a trivial thing for him
to walk in the sins of Jeroboam the son of Nebat, that he married Jezebel the daughter of Ethbaal King of the Sidonians, and
went to serve Baal and worshipped him." (32) "So, he erected
an altar for Baal in the house of Baal, which he built in Samaria.
(33) "And Ahab also made the Asherah, thus Ahab did more to
provoke the Lord God of Israel than all the Kings of Israel who
were before him."

But you have read in 1 Kings 16:31-33 - Ahab, son of
Omri, Omri (Pupil of Jehovah) Originally captain of the host to
Elah, was afterward himself King of Israel, and founder of the
third dynasty, (926BC). After the death of Elah, they proclaimed
Omri King. Ahab married Jezebel, daughter of Ethbaal, King of
Tyre. Ahad, the King of Israel, married Jezebel of Tyre, a cel-
ebrated commercial city of Phoenicia. Ahab, in obedience to her
wishes, caused him to build a tempt to Baal, the name of a
Phoenician god or rather of the idols itself, the supreme male
divinity of Phoenician and Canaanite nations. Ashtoreth (a
Star) was their supreme female divinity. God said for them not
marry heathen and to be separate from them, but Ahab married

Jezebel who was a Phoenician princess, the daughter of Ethbaal, King of the Zidonians. The Phoenicians were idolaters, and worshipped Ashtoreth, the Star. They burned children as sacrifice to a Phoenician god.

New International, Judges 10:6 "Again the Israelites did evil in the eyes of the Lord. They served the Baal and the Ashtoreths, and the gods of Aram, the god of Sidon, the god of Moab, the gods of the Ammonite and the gods of the Philistines and because the Israelite forsook the Lord and no longer served Him.

Now you read Judges 10:6 "Now you can see all the gods that Israel served, they were to serve only and worship god and obey a Holy God and walk with Him through obedience to His laws, and be separate from other Gods, and from heathen nations, and fellowship with Him through sacrifice, and offerings. But they forsook the Lord God, did not keep His laws nor His covenant or ordinances. This is the reason God said return. "You have robbed Me of tithes and offerings." The nation of Israel robbed Him because they stopped serving Him.

Same Ref. The Philistines appear to have been deeply imbued with superstition, they carried their idols with them on their campaigns. 2 Sam. 5:21 - and proclaimed their victories in their presence. 1 Sam 31:9 - The gods whom they chiefly worshipped were Dagon, Judges 16:23, 1 Sam. 5:3-5, 1Chron. 10:10 - Ashtaroth, 1 Sam. 31:10 - Herod.1.105, and Baalzeeb, 2 Kings 2:6 — read those verses.

Ref. Smith Bible Dic., page 133 - The Israelites also worshipped, alongside with the Philistines, Dagon the Fish god, apparently the masculine. 1 Sam. 5:3-4 - correlative of Atargatis, was the national god of the Philistines. The most famous temples of Dagon were at Gaza, Judges 16:21-30 - and Ashdod, 1 Sam. 5:5-6. 1 Chron. 10:10. The latter temple was destroyed by Jonathan in the Maccabaean wars. Traces of the worship of Dagon likewise appear in the name Caphar-dagon (Near Jamnia) and Beth-dagon in Judah, Josh. 15:41, and Asher. Josh. 19:27. Dagon was represented with the face and hands of a man and the tail of a fish. 1 Sam. 5:5. The fish-like form was a natural emblem of fruitfulness, and as such was likely to be adopted by seafaring tribes in the representation of their gods.

Ref. Smith Bible Dic., page 216 - Gideon was the fifth recorded Judge of Israel and for many reasons the greatest of them all. He was called to be a deliverer, and he destroyed Baal's altar.

Jud. 8:33 - then it came about as soon as Gideon was dead, that the sons of Israel again played the Harlot, with Baal, and made Baalberith their god. They the nation of Israel, is the nation God is saying, "Return to Me, you are robbing Me of tithes and offerings. He was speaking to that nation.

Now you have seen what God did to Israel in Num. 25:4 - You have seen how God's fierce anger came against Israel for disobeying Him and serving idols.

2 Kings 1-3: "Now Moab rebelled against Israel after the death of Ahab. Ahab, the son of Omri, served as King of Israel."

2 Kings 1:2 "And Ahaziah feel through the lattice in his upper chamber which was in Samaria, and because ill, so he sent messengers and said to them, Go, inquire of Baal-zebub, the god of Ekron, whether I shall recover from this sickness.

Ahaziah, the son of Ahab, and Jezebel, eighth King of Israel, sent to inquire of Baal-zebub, an idols, worshipped by the heathen nations.

2 Kings 1:3 "But the angel of the Lord said to Elijah the Tishbite, Arise, go up to meet the messengers of King of Samaria and say to them, Is it because there is not God in Israel that you are going to inquire of Baal-zebub, the god of Ekron? Baal-zebub - lord of the Philistines."

2 Kings 1:4 "Now therefore thus says the Lord, You shall not come down from the bed where you have gone up, but you shall surely die. Then Elijah departed."

Jer. 7:18 "The children gather wood, and the fathers kindle the fire, and the women knead dough to make cakes for the queen of heaven, and they pour out libations to other gods in order to spite Me."

Jer. 7:30 "They the people of Judah have done evil in My eyes, declares the Lord. They have set up their detestable idol in the house that bears My name and have defiled it." (30) This is why they stopped paying their tithes and offerings, they set up their own gods to worship and turned from God to idols.

Here are things they did to stop paying tithes and offerings to God

Jer. 7:31 "And they have built high places of Topheth, which in the valley of the son of Hinnom, to burn their sons and their daughters in the fire, which I did not command, and it did not come into My mind.

2 Kings 17:8 "And they walked in the customs of the nation whom the Lord had driven out before the sons of Israel, and in the customs of the Kings of Israel which they introduced.

2 Kings 17:9 "And the sons of Israel did things secretly which were not right against the Lord their God. Moreover, they built for themselves high places all their towns, from watchtower to fortified city."

2 Kings 17:9 - Living Bible - "The people of Israel had also secretly done many things that were wrong, and they had built altars to other gods throughout the land."

2 Kings 17:10 "And they set up sacred stone and Asherah poles on every hill and under every spreading tree." Ref. New International Bible.

Ref. Smith Bible Dic., page 58 - The Israelites set up Asherah in 2 Kings 17:10 - Asherah was the name of a Phoenician goddess, or rather of the idol itself (Authorized Version). Asherah is closely connected with Ashtoreth and her worship. Judges 3:7 comp. 2:3 Judges, 6:25 - 1 Kings 18:19 - Ashtoreth being, perhaps, the proper name of the goddess, whilst Asherah is the name of her image or symbol, which was of wood. See Judges 6:25-30, 2 Kings 23:14, page 60 - Asherah is closely associated with Ashtoreth, and he worshipped Ashtoreth was a star, the principle female divinity of the Phoenicians, called Ishtar by the Assyrians, and Astarte by the Greeks and Romans. She was, by some ancient writers, identified with the moon. But on the other hand, the Assyrian Ishtar was not the moon goddess, but the planet Venus, and Astarte was by many identified with the goddess Venus or Aphrodite, as well as with the planet of that name. It is certain that the worship of Astarte became identified with that of Venus, and that this worship was connected with the most impure rites is apparent from the close connection of this goddess with Asherah, 1 Kings 11:5, 33 - 2 Kings 23:13.

Mal. 3:8 "From the days of your fathers you have turned aside from My statutes and have not kept them. Return unto Me, and I will return to you, says the Lord of Hosts. But you say, How shall we return? Will a man rob God? But you say, how have we robbed Thee? Yet, you are robbing Me in tithes, and offerings."

God said in Ex. 20:4 "You shall not make for yourself an idol, or any likeness of what is in heaven above or on the earth beneath or in the water under the earth."

Ex. 20:3 "You shall have no other gods before Me."

Lev. 19:4 "Do not turn to idols or make yourselves molten gods. I am the Lord your God."

Ex. 20:4 "You shall not worship them or serve them, for I, the Lord your God, am a jealous God, visiting the iniquity of the father on the children, on the third and the fourth generations of those who hate Me."

Ex. 20:23 "You shall not make other gods besides Me, gods of silver or gods of gold, you shall not make for yourselves."

Deu. 26:17 "You have today declared the Lord to be your God, and that you would walk in His ways and keep His statutes, His commandments and His ordinances, and listen to His voice."

God said for the Israelites not to marry heathen or worship their idols, and be separated from them. Now read Gen. 41:50-52. You will see that Joseph son of Jacob whose name was changed to Israel, married Asenath (worship of Neith), the daughter of Potiphear, a priest of On. Potiphera, his daughter, was given to Joseph to wife by Pharaoh King of Egypt. Gen. 41:45-50 —46-20BC On (Abode or city of the Sun) a town of lower Egypt, called Beth-Shemesh in Jer. 43:13. On is better known under its Greek name Heliopolis; the chief object of worship at Heliopolis was sun.

Gen. 41: "And Joseph named the first-born Manasseh, for he said, God has made Me forget all my troubles and all my father's household."

Gen. 41:52 " And he named the second Ephraim, for he said, God has made me fruitful in the land of my affliction."

Hosea 13:1 "When Ephraim spoke, there was trembling. He exalted himself in Israel. But through Baal he did wrong and died."

Ephraim worshipped Baal, an idol God said not to serve or worship.

Hosea 11:2 "The more they called them, the more they went from them, they kept sacrificing to Baal and burning incense to idols."

Jer. 18:15 "For My people have forgotten Me. They burn incense to worthless gods, and they have stumbled from their ways."

God said in Lev. 19:4 "Do not turn to idols or make for yourselves molten gods, I am the Lord your God." But you see what they did in Hosea 13:2, "And now they sin more and more, and make for themselves molten images, idols skillfully made of craftsmen. They say of them. Let the men who sacrifices kiss the calves."

Hosea 11:1-2 "When Israel was a youth I loved him and out of Egypt I called My son."

Hosea 9-10 "I found Israel like grapes in the wilderness. I saw your forefathers as earliest fruit on the fig tree in its first season. But they came to Baal-peor and devoted themselves to shame. And they became as detestable as that which they loved."

Jer. 7:9 "Will you steal, murder, and commit adultery and swear falsely, and offer sacrifice to Baal, and walk after other gods that you have not known?"

Ex. 20:3 "You shall have no other gods before Me."

Jer. 7:10 "Then come and stand before Me in this house, which is called by My name, and say, We are delivered, that you may do all these abominations."

Jer. 7:11 "Has this house, which is called by My name, become a den of robbers in your sight? Behold, I have seen it declares the Lord."

Ezek. 23:35 "Therefore thus says the Lord God, because you have forgotten Me and cast Me behind your back, bear now the punishment of your lewdness and your harlotries."

Ezek. 23:36 "Moreover, the Lord said to Me, Son of Man, will you judge Oholah and Oholibah? Then declare to them their abominations."

Ezek. 23:37 "For they have committed adultery, and blood is on their hands. Thus they have committed adultery with their idols and even caused their sons, whom they bore to Me, to pass through the fire to them as food."

Ezek. 5:11 "So as I live, declares the Lord God, surely because you have defiled My sanctuary with all your detestable idols and with all your abominations, therefore I will also withdraw, and My eye shall have no pity and I will not spare."

Ezek. 23:39 "For when they had slaughtered their children for their idols, they entered My sanctuary on the same day to profane it, and lo, thus they did within My house."

Jer. 18:15 "For My people have forgotten Me, they burned incense to worthless gods and they have stumbled from their ways."

Hosea 4:12 "My people consult their wooden idols and their diviner's wand informs them; for a spirit of harlotry has led them astray and they have played the harlot, departing from their God."

Jud. 10:10 "Then the sons of Israel cried out to the Lord, saying, we have sinned against Thee, for indeed, we have forsaken our God and served the Baal."

Sam. 12:10 "and they cried out to the Lord and said, we have sinned because we have forsaken the Lord and have served the Baals and Ashtaroth, but now deliver us from the hands of our enemies, and we will serve Thee."

Ex. 34:15-16 "Lest you make a covenant with the inhabitants of the land and they play the harlot with their gods, and sacrifice to their gods, and some one invites you to eat of his sacrifice."

Ex. 34:16 "And you take some of his daughters for your sons, and his daughters play the harlot with their gods."

Num. 25:1 "While Israel remained at Shittim, the people began to play the harlot with the daughters of Moab."

Num. 25:2 "For they invited the people to the sacrifice of their gods, and the people eat and bowed down to their gods."

Num. 25:3 "So Israel joined themselves to Baal of Peor, and the Lord was angry against Israel."

Num. 31:16 "Behold, these caused the sons of Israel, through the counsel of Balaam, to trespass against the Lord in the matter of Peor, so the plague was among the congregation of the Lord."

Ezek. 48:11 "It shall be for the priests who are sanctified of the sons of Zadok, who have kept My charge, who did not go astray when the sons of Israel went astray, as the Levites went astray."

Ezek. 44:10 "But the Levites who went far from Me when Israel went astray who went astray from Me after their idols, shall bear the punishment for their iniquity."

When God said "Return unto Me, you have robbed Me out of tithes and offerings, He was saying to the Israelites of Israel." In Ex. 20:4 "You shall not make for yourself any idols. Ex. 20:3 "You shall have no other God before Me." Ex. 20:5 "You shall not worship them." But in Hosea 4:12 - They made wooden idols, an idol is anything used as an object of worship in the place of the true God. They made wooden idols and diviners, and played harlot, which God said for them not to worship any other god. A harlot in Hosea 4:12 - is a woman who is promiscuous, a prostitute.

God called the Levites from among the sons of Israel to serve as priests, to perform the duties of the congregation before the tent meeting, to do the same of the Tabernacle, in Ezek. 48:11 "It is for the priests, that is the sons of Zadok, who obey Me and didn't go into sin when the people of Israel and the rest of their tribe of Levi. did." (12) Because they ministered unto them before their idols, and caused the house of Israel to fall into iniquity; therefore have I lifted up mine hand against them, saith the Lord God, and they shall bear their iniquity but because they encouraged the people to worship other gods, causing Israel to fall into deep sin. I have raised My hand and taken oath, says the Lord God, that they must be punished. (13) They shall not come near Me to minister as priests; they may not touch any of My holy things, for they must bear their shame for all the sins they have committed."

"For when they had slaughtered their children for their idols, they entered My sanctuary on the same day to profane it, and lo, thus they did within My house."

Ezek 20:6 "On that day I swore to them, to bring them out from the land of Egypt into a land that I had selected for them, flowing with milk and honey which is the glory of all lands."

Ezek. 20:7 "And I said to them, Cast away, each of you, the detestable things of his eyes, and do not defile yourselves with the idols of Egypt, I am the Lord your God."

Ezek. 20:8 "But they rebelled against Me and were not willing to listen to Me. They did not cast away the detestable things of their eyes, nor did they forsake the idols of Egypt."

Ezek. 20:13 "But the house of Israel rebelled against Me in the wilderness. They did not walk in My statutes, and they rejected My ordinances, by which if a man observes them he will live, and My sabbath they greatly profaned. Then I resolved to pour out My wrath on them in the wilderness, to annihilate them."

Ezek. 20:16 "Because they rejected My ordinances, and as for My statutes, they did not walk in them, they even profaned My sabbath, for their hearts continually went after their idols."

Ezek. 20:18 "And I said to their children in the wilderness, do not walk in the statutes of your father, or keep ordinances, or defile yourselves with their idols."

Ezek. 20:19 "I am the Lord your God, walk in My statutes and keep My ordinances, and observe them."

Ezek. 20:20 "And sanctify My sabbath, and they shall be a sign between Me and you, that you may know that I am the Lord your God."

Ezek. 14:3-4 "Son of man, these men have set up their idols in their hearts, and have put right before their faces the stumbling block of their iniquity. Should I be consulted by them all."

Ezek. 8:5 "Then He said to Me, son of man, raise your eyes now toward the north. So I raised my eyes toward the north, and behold, to the north of the altar gate was this idol of jealousy at the entrance."

Jer. 7:31 "And they have built the high place of Topheth, which is in the valley of the son of Hinnom, to burn their sons and their daughters in the fire, which I did not command and it did not come into My mind."

Jer. 7:30 "For the sons of Judah have done that which is evil in My sight, declares the Lord, they have set their detestable things in the house which is called by My name, to defile it."

In Num. 25:1 - Shittim was the place of Israel's encampment between the conquest of the Transjordanic highlands and the passage of the Jordan. Moab was the son of Lot's eldest daughter, the progenitor of the Moabites. The religion of the Moabites was the fire-god Molech, the tutelary deity of the children of Ammon, and essentially identical with the Moabitish Chemosh. Fire gods appear to have been common to all the Canaanite, Syrian and Arab tribes, who worship the destructive element under an outward symbol with the most inhuman rites. According to Jewish tradition, the image of Molech was of brass, hollow within, and was situated without Jerusalem. His face was that of a calf, and his hands stretched forth like a man who opens his hands to receive some thing of his neighbor. "And they kindled it with fire and the priest took the babe and put it into the hands of Molech, and the babe gave up the ghost." Ref. Smith Bible Dic., page 411 for Moab, page 413 for Molech-Shittim, page 625 for Shittim.

Ref. Smith Bible Dic., page 113 - Chemosh, the national Deity of the Moabites, he also appears as the god of the Ammonites. These were the gods of Israel bowed down to worshipped. This is why God said in Malachi 3:7-8 "Return unto Me, You are robbing Me of tithes and offerings." God said to them in Ex. 20:3 - that they shall have no other gods before Him. In Ex. 20:5 "You shall not worship them nor serve them." But they turned from God to worship and serve other gods; this is why they stopped bringing their tithes, and offerings to Him. They turned from Him.

Num. 25:2 "For they invited the people to the sacrifice of their gods, and the people ate and bowed down to their God."

Num. 25:3 "So Israel joined themselves to Baal of Peor, and the Lord was angry against Israel."

Jer. 44:3 "Because of their wickedness which they committed so as to provoke Me to anger by continuing to burn sacrifices and to serve other gods whom they had not known neither they, you nor your fathers."

Jer. 44:4 "Yet I sent you all My servants the prophets, again and again, saying Oh, do not do this abominable thing which I hate."

Jer. 44:5 "But they did not listen or incline their ear to turn from their wickedness, so as not to burn sacrifice to other gods."

Here are scriptures to show you that they continued in their wickedness by continuing to turn from God and serve other gods.

Jer. 44:15 "Then all the men who were aware that their wives were burning sacrifice to other gods, along with all the women who were standing by, as a large assembly, including all the people who were living in Pathros in the land of Egypt, responded to Jeremiah saying."

Jer. 44:16 "As for the message that you have spoken to us in the name of the Lord, we are not going to listen to you."

Jer. 44:17 - "But rather we will certainly carry out every word that has proceeded from our mouths, by burning sacrifices to queen of heaven and pouring out libations to her just as we ourselves our forefathers, our Kings and our princes did in the cities of Judah and in the streets of Jerusalem, for then we had plenty of food, and were well off, and saw no misfortune."

Jer. 44:23 "Because you have burned sacrifices and have sinned against the Lord and not obeyed the voice of the Lord or walked in His law, His statutes or His testimonies, therefore this calamity has befallen you, as it has this day."

Jer. 44:19 "And, said the women, when we were burning sacrifices to the queen of heaven, and pouring out libations to her, was it without our husbands that we made for her sacrificial cakes in her image and poured out libations to her?" Libations means, a pouring out of wine or other liquid in honor of a deity, the ceremonial practice of the ancient Greeks and Romans.

Jer. 32:29 "And the Chaldeans who are fighting against this city shall enter and set this city on fire and burn it, with the house where people have offered incense to Baal on their roofs and poured out libations to other gods to provoke Me to anger."

Jer. 32:29 - They robbed God, out of tithes and offerings, when they, in Jer. 32:29, offered incense to Baal. Incense is an aromatic gum or other substance, producing a sweet odor when burned, used especially in religious ceremonies.

More Scriptures to show you how Israel turned from God.

2 Chron. 36:19 "Then they burned the house of God, and broke down the wall of Jerusalem and burned all its fortified buildings with fire, and destroyed all its valuable articles."

Jer. 32:30 "Indeed the sons of Israel and the sons of Judah have been doing only evil in My sight from their youth, for the sons of Israel have been only provoking Me to anger by the work of their hands, declares dhe Lord."

Jer. 32:31 "Indeed this city has been to Me a provocation of My anger and My wrath from the day that they built it, even to this day, that it should be removed from before My face."

Jer. 32:32 "Because of all the evil of the sons of Israel and the sons of Judah, which they have done to provoke Me to anger - they, their Kings, their leaders, their priest, their prophets, the men of Judah, and the inhabitants of Jerusalem."

Jer. 32:33 "And they have turned their back to Me, and not their face; though I taught them; teaching again and again, they would not listen and receive instruction."

Jer. 32:34 "But they put their detestable things in the house which is called by My name to defile it."

Jer. 32:35 "And they built the high places of Baal that are in the valley of Beb-hinnom to cause their sons and their daughters to pass through the fire of Molech, which I had not commanded them nor had it entered My mind that they should do this abomination, to cause Judah to sin."

Jer. 19:4 "Because they have forsaken Me and made this an alien place and have burned sacrifices in it to other gods that neither they nor their forefathers nor the Kings of Judah have ever known, and because they have filled this place with the blood of the innocent."

Jer. 19:5 "And have built the high places of Baal to burn their sons, in the fire as burnt offerings to Baal, a thing which I never commanded or spoke of, nor did it ever enter My mind."

Jer. 16:11 "Then you are to say to them, it is because your forefathers have forsaken Me, declares the Lord, and have followed other gods and served them and bowed down to them; but Me they have forsaken and have not kept My law."

Jer. 16:12 "You too have done evil, even more than your forefathers; for behold, you are each one walking according to the stubbornness of his own evil heart, without listening to Me."

2 Kings 21:6 "And he made his son pass through the fire, practiced witchcraft and used divination, and dealt with medi-

ums and spiritists. He did much evil in sight of the Lord provoking Him to anger."

Here are more scriptures to show that
they continued to rob God

2 Chron. 34:24 "Thus says the Lord, Behold, I am bringing evil on this place and on its inhabitants, even all curses written in the book which they have read in the presence of the King of Judah."

2 Chron. 34:25 "Because they have forsaken Me and have provoked Me and burned incense to other gods, that they might provoke Me to anger with all the works of their hands, therefore My wrath will be poured out on this place, and it shall not be quenched."

2 Chron. 33:1 "Manasseh was twelve years old when he became King, and he reigned fifty-five years in Jerusalem."

2 Chron. 33:2 "And he did evil in the sight of the Lord according to the abomination of the nations whom the Lord dispossessed before the sons of Israel."

2 Chron. 33:3 "For he rebuilt the high places which Hezekiah his father had broken down, he also erected altars for Baal and made Asherim, and worshipped all the hosts of heaven and served them."

2 Chron. 33:4 "And he built altars in the house of the Lord of which the Lord had said, My name shall be in Jerusalem forever."

2 Chron. 33:5 "For he built altars for all the hosts of heaven in the two courts of the house of the Lord."

2 Chron. 33:6 "and he made his sons pass through the fire in the valley of Benhinnom, and he practiced witchcraft, used divination, practiced sorcery, and dealt with mediums and spiritists. He did much evil in the sight of the Lord, provoking Him to anger."

2 Kings 21:1 "Manasseh was twelve years old when he became King, and he reigned fifty-five years in Jerusalem, and his mother's name was Hephzibah."

2 Kings 21:2 "And he did evil in the sight of the Lord, according to the abominations of the nations whom the Lord dispossessed before the sons of Israel."

2 Kings 21:3 "For he rebuilt the high place which Hezekiah his father had destroyed, and he erected altars for Baal and made an Asherah, as Ahab King of Israel had done, and worshipped all the hosts of heaven and served them. Heaven's host was a wooden symbol of a female deity, an image."

2 Kings 21:4 "And he built an altar in the house of the Lord, of which the Lord had said, in Jerusalem I will put My name."

2 Kings 21:5 "For he built altars for all the hosts of heaven in the two courts of the house of the Lord."

2 Kings 21:6 "And he made his sons pass through the fire, practiced witchcraft and used divination, and dealt with mediums and spiritists; he did much evil in the sight of the Lord provoking Him to anger."

2 Kings 21:7 "Then he set the carved image of Asherah that he had made in the house of which the Lord said to David and to his son Solomon. In this house and in Jerusalem, which I have chosen from all the tribes of Israel, I will put My name forever."

2 Kings 21:9 "But they did not listen, and Manasseh seduced them to do evil more than the nations whom the Lord destroyed before the sons of Israel."

2 Kings 21:10-11 "Now the Lord spoke through His servants the prophets, saying (11) Because Manasseh King of Judah has done these abominations, having done wickedly more than all the Amorites did who were before him, and has also made Judah sin with his idols."

138

Here are more scriptures to show you that Israel stopped serving God. This is why God said in Mal. 3:7-8 "Return unto Me, you are robbing Me of tithes and offerings." These scriptures will show you that they went and served other gods. He said in Ex. 20:3 "That you shall have no other gods before Me." This is the reason they stopped paying their tithes and offerings.

2 Kings 17:7 "Now this came about, because the sons of Israel had sinned against the Lord their God, who had brought them up from the land of Egypt from under the hands of Pharaoh, king of Egypt, and they had feared other gods.

2 Kings 17:8 "And walked in the customs of the nations whom the Lord had driven out before the sons of Israel, and in the customs of the kings of Israel which they had introduced."

2 Kings 17:9 "And the sons of Israel did things secretly which were not right, against the Lord their God. Moreover, they built for themselves high places in all their towns, from watchtower to fortified city."

2 Kings 17:10 "And they set for themselves sacred pillars and Asherim on every high hill and under every green tree."

2 Kings 17:11 "And there they burned incense on all the high places as the nations did which the Lord had carried away to exile before them; and they did evil things provoking the Lord."

2 Kings 17:12 "And they served idols, concerning which the Lord had said to them, you shall not do this thing."

2 Kings 17:13 "Yet the Lord warned Israel and Judah, through all His prophets and every seer, saying Turn from your evil ways and keep My commandments, My statutes, according to all he law which I commanded your fathers, and which I sent to you through My servants the prophets."

2 Kings 17:14 "However, they did not listen, but stiffened their necks like their fathers, who did not believe in the Lord their God."

2 Kings 17:15 "And they rejected His statutes and His covenant which He made with their fathers, and His warning with which he warned them. And they followed vanity and became vain, and went after the nations which surrounded them, concerning which the Lord had commanded them not to do like them."

2 Kings 17:16 "And they forsook all the commandments of the Lord their God and made for themselves molten images, even two calves, and made an Asherah and worshipped all the hosts of heaven and served Baal."

2 Kings 17:17 "Then they made their sons and daughters pass through the fire, and practiced divination and enchantments, and sold themselves to do evil in the sight of the Lord, provoking Him."

God said in Deu. 26:17 "You have today declared the Lord to be your God, and that you would walk in His ways, and keep His statutes, His commandments and His ordinances, and listen to His voice." But they didn't listen to His voice nor did they keep His law or His statutes nor His commandments, or His ordinances. They turned from God and they walked in the customs of the nations whom the Lord had driven out before the sons of Israel. In 2 Kings 17:9 - They turned from God to do secretly things which were not right, they built for themselves high places in all their towns. Ref. Smith Bible Dic., page 247 - From the earliest times it was the custom among all nations to erect altars and places of worship on lofty and conspicuous spots. Now-with-standing this, we find that it was implicitly forbidden by the law of Moses, Deu. 12:11-14, which also gave the strictest injuction to destroy these monuments of Canaanite idolatry, Lev. 26.

2 Kings 17:25 "And it came about at the beginning of their living there, that they did not fear the Lord, therefore the Lord sent lions among them which killed some of them."

2 Kings 17:26 "So they spoke to the King of Assyria, saying, the nation whom you have carried away into exile in the cities of Samaria do not know the custom of the god of the land, so he has sent lions among them, and behold, they killed them because they do not know the custom of the god of the land."
2 Kings 17:27 "Then the King of Assyria commanded, saying, Take there one of the priests whom you carried away into exile, and let him go and live there, and let him teach them the custom of the god of the land."
2 Kings 17:28 "So one of the priests whom they had carried away into exile from Samaria came and lived at Bethel, and taught them how they should fear the Lord."
2 Kings 17:29 "But every nation still made gods of its own and put them in the house of the high places which the people of Samaria had made, every nation in their cities in which they lived."
God says in Lev. 26:30 - "I then will destroy your high places and cut down your incense altars and heap your remains on the remains of your idols for My soul shall abhor you." But in 2 Kings 17:11 - They turned from God's statutes and didn't walk in His ways nor did they practice His statutes were they holy.
1 Kings 14:9 "And also have done more evil than all who were before you and have made for yourself other gods, and molten images to provoke Me to anger and have cast me behind your back."
1 Kings 12:28 "So the King consulted, and made two golden calves, and he said to them. It is too much for you to go up to Jerusalem: behold your gods, O Israel, that brought you up from the land of Egypt."
1 Kings 16:32 "So he erected an altar for Baal in the house of Baal, which he built in Samaria."
1 Kings 16:33 "And Ahab also made Asherah. Thus Ahab did more to provoke the Lord God of Israel than all the Kings

of Israel who were before him."

1 Kings 11:1 "Now King Solomon loved many foreign women along with the daughter of Pharaoh, Moabite, Ammonite, Edomite, Sidonian, and Hittite women."

Neh. 13:23 "In those days I saw that the Jews had married women from Ashdob, Ammon, and Moab."

1 Kings 11:2 "From the nations concerning which the Lord had said to the sons of Israel, You shall not associate with them, neither shall they associate with you, for they will surely turn your heart away after their gods." Solomon held fast to these in love.

1 Kings 11:3 "and he had seven hundred wives, princesses, and three hundred concubines, and his wives turned his heart away.

1 Kings 11:4 "For it came about when Solomon was old his wives turned his heart away after other gods; and his heart was not wholly devoted to the Lord his God, as the heart of David his father had been."

1 Kings 11:5 "For Solomon went after Ashtoreth the goddess of the Sidonians and after Milcom the detestable idols of the Ammonites."

1 Kings 11:6 "And Solomon did what was evil in the sight of the Lord, and did not follow the Lord fully, as David his father had done."

1 Kings 11:7 "Then Solomon built a high place for Chemosh the detestable idol of Moah, on the mountain which is east of Jerusalem, and for Molech the detestable idol of the sons of Ammon."

Neh. 13:24 "As for their children, half spoke in the language of Ashdob, and none of them was able to speak the language of Judah, but the language of his own people."

Neh. 13:25 "So I contended with them and cursed them and stuck some of them and pulled out their hair, and made them swear by God. You shall not give your daughter to their sons, nor take of their daughters for your sons of for yourselves."

Neh. 13:26 "Did not Solomon King of Israel sin regarding these things. Yet among the nations there was no King like him, and he was loved by his God and God made him King over all Israel, nevertheless the foreign women caused even him to sin."

God said in Deu. 7:2-4 "You shall make no covenant with them and show no favor to them. (3) Furthermore, you shall not intermarry with them; you shall not give your daughters to their sons, nor shall you take their daughters for your sons. (4) For they will turn your sons away from following Me." But Solomon went and formed a marriage alliance with Pharaoh King of Egypt, and took Pharaoh's daughter and brought her to the city of David, until he had finished building his own house and the house of the Lord and the wall around Jerusalem in 1 Kings 3:1 - when God said in 1 Kings 11:2 "From the nations concerning which the Lord had said to the sons of Israel, You shall not associate with them, neither shall they associate with you, for they will surely turn your heart away after their gods, Solomon held fast to these in love.

1 Kings 11:33 "Because they have forsaken Me, and have worshipped Ashtoreth the goddess of the Sidonians, Chemosh the god of Ammon; and they have not walked in My ways, doing what is right in My sight and observing My statutes and My ordinances, as his father David did."

1 Samuel 7:3 "Then Samuel spoke to all the house of Israel, saying, If you return to the Lord with all your heart, remove the foreign gods and the Ashtaroth from among you and direct your heart to the Lord and serve Him alone; and He will deliver you from the hand of the Philistines."

1 Samuel 12:10 "And they cried out to the Lord and said, we have sinned because we have forsaken the Lord and have served the Baals and the Ashtaroth; but now deliver us from the hands of our enemies, and we will serve Thee."

Judges 2:13 "So they forsook the Lord and served Baal and the Ashtaroth."

Judges 2:17 "And yet they did not listen to their Judges, for they played the harlot after other gods and bowed themselves down to them. They turned aside quickly from the way in which their fathers had walked in obeying the commandments of the Lord. They did not do as their father."

Judges 2:19 "But it came about when the judge died, that they would turn back and act more corruptly than their fathers, in following other gods to serve them and bow down to them; they did not abandon their practices or their stubborn ways."

Judges 3:7 "And the sons of Israel did what was evil in the sight of the Lord, and forgot the Lord their God, and served the Baals and the Ashtaroth."

Judges 10:6 "Then the sons of Israel again did evil in the sight of the Lord, served the Baals and the Ashtaroth, the gods of Aram, the gods of Sidon, the gods of Moab, the gods of the Philistines; thus they forsook the Lord and did not serve Him."

Judges 10:10 "Then the sons of Israel cried out to the Lord, saying we have sinned against Thee, for indeed, we have forsaken our Lord and served the Baals."

Judges 10:13 "Yet you have forsaken Me and served other gods; therefore I will deliver you no more."

Deu. 29:26 "And they went and served other gods and worshipped them, gods whom they have not known and whom He had not allotted to them."

When God said in Mal. 3:12 "And all the nations will call you blessed, for you shall be a delightful land, says the Lord of Hosts." Cross Ref. Isa. 61:9, Isa. 62:4.

This is what God means by them being blessed. Our churches are using this scripture to say God is speaking about us.

When God said in Mal. 3:10-12 -To bring the tithes into the storehouse. "If I will not open for you the windows of heaven, and then I will rebuke the devourer for you, and all nations will call you blessed, for you shall be a delightful land." Cross Ref. on tithes-Lev. 27:30.

This is what God means by them being blessed. Cross Ref. on Malachi 3:12 go to Isa. 61:9 and 62:4.

Isa. 61:9 "Then their offspring will be known among the nations, and their descendants in the midst of the peoples, all who see them will recognize them because they are the offspring whom the Lord has blessed."

Isa. 44:3 "For I will pour out water on the thirsty land, and streams on the dry ground: I will pour out My spirit on your offspring, and my blessing on your descendants and they will spring up among the grass like poplars by streams of water."

Joel 2:28 "And it will come about after this that I will pour out My Spirit on all mankind and your sons and daughters will prophesy, you old men will see visions."

Isa. 32:15 "Until the Spirit is poured out upon us from on high, and the wilderness becomes a fertile field. And the fertile field is considered a forest."

Isa. 29:17 "Is it yet just a little while, before Lebanon will be turned in to a fertile field, and the field will be considered as a forest."

Isa. 35:1 "The wilderness and the desert will be glad, and the Arab will rejoice and blossom; (2) It will blossom profusely, and rejoice with rejoicing and shouts of joy, the majesty of our Lord."

Isa. 41:18 "I will open rivers on the bare heights, and springs in the midst of the valleys; I will make the wilderness a pool of water, and the dry land a fountain of water." (19) "I will put the cedar in the wilderness, the acacia, and the myrtle and the olive tree, I will place the juniper in the desert, together with the box tree and the cypress. (20) That they may see and recognize, and consider and gain insight as well that the hand of the

Lord has done this, and the Holy One of Israel has created it."

Isa. 27:10 "For the fortified city is isolated, a homestead forlorn and forsaken like the desert; there the calf will graze, and there it will lie down and feed on its branches."

Isa. 51:3 "Indeed, the Lord will comfort Zion; he will comfort all her waste place, and her wilderness He will make like Eden, and her desert like the garden of the Lord; Joy and gladness will be found in her, Thanksgiving and sound of a melody."

Isa. 62:4 "It will no longer be said to you, 'Forsaken,' nor to you land will it any longer be said, 'desolate.' But you will be called, "My delight is in her, and your land, married, for the Lord delights in you, and to Him your land will be married."

Jer. 32:41 "For I will rejoice over them to do them good, and I will faithfully plant them in this land with all My heart and with all My soul. (42) For thus says the Lord, Just as I brought all this great disaster on this people, so I am going to bring on them all the good that I am promising them."

These were things that God said He would do for them if they would return unto him, and keep his statutes, and his ordinances, and his commandments. He would rebuke the devourer from their ground, and all nations will call them blessed and they shall be a delightful land says the Lord of Hosts.

Chapter 11

Here are some covenants God made with man.

The Edenic Covenant

Gen. 2:17 - The covenant in Eden is the first of the general or universal covenants. In it Adam is charged to: (a) populate the earth (Gen. 1:28); (b) subdue the earth (1-28); (c) exercise dominion over the animal creation (Gen. 1:28); (d) care for the garden of Eden and enjoy its fruit (Gen. 1:29 and 2:15); and (e) refrain from eating the fruit of the tree of the knowledge of good and evil, under penalty of death (Gen. 2:16-17). The Edenic Covenant was terminated by man's disobedience when Adam and Eve ate of the fruit of the tree of the knowledge of good and evil, resulting in their spiritual and physical death. This failure necessitated the establishment of the covenant with Adam. (Page 9 - Gen. 3:14-21).

The Adamic Covenant

Gen. 3:14-21 - The covenant with Adam is the second general or universal covenant. It could be called the covenant with mankind, for its sets forth the conditions which will hold sway until the curse of sin is lifted. (cf, page, 762 - Isa. 11:6-10, page 1299 - Rom. 8:18-23). According to the covenant, the conditions which will prevail are.

    a. The serpent, the tool used by Satan to effect the fall of man, is cursed. The curse affects not only the instrumen the serpent, but also the indwelling energizer, Satan. Great physical changes took place in the serpent. Apparently, it was upright, now it will go on its belly (14). It was the most desirable animal of the animal creation. Now it is the most loathsome. The sight or thought of a snake should be an effective reminder of the devastating effects of sin.

    b. Satan is judged, he will enjoy limited success (you shall bruise his head) (15), but ultimately he will be judged (he shall bruise your heel).

    c. The first prophecy of the coming of Messiah is given (15).

    d. There will be a multiplication of conception, necessitated by the introduction of death into the human race. (16).

    e. There will be a pain in childbirth (16).

    f. The woman is made subject to her husband. (16).

    g. The ground is cursed and will bring forth weeds among the food which man must eat for his existence (17-19)

    h. Physical changes take place in man, he will perspire when he works, he will have to work all his life long (19).

    i. In sinning, man dies spiritually, and ultimately will die physically. His body will decay until it returns to the du from which it was originally taken (19). Now turn to page, 14 - Gen. 9:1-9.

Gen. 9:1-19 - The Noahic Covenant

The Covenant with Noah is the third general or universal covenant. Noah has just passed through the universal flood in which all the world's population has been wiped out. Only Noah, his wife, his three sons, and their wives - eight people - constitute the world's population. Noah might have thought that the things provided by the covenant with Adam had now been changed. However, God give the Noahic Covenant so that Noah and all the human race to follow might know that the provisions made in the Adamic Covenant remain in effect with one notable addition, the principle of human government which includes the responsibility of suppressing the outbreak of sin and violence, so that it will not be necessary to destroy the earth again by a flood. The provisions of the Covenant are:

a. The responsibility to populate the earth is reaffirmed (1),
b.The subjection of the animal kingdom to man is reaffirmed (2),
c.Man is permitted to eat the flesh of animals. However, he is to refrain from consuming blood. (3-4),
d. The sacredness of human life is established. Whatever sheds man's blood, whether man or beast, must be put to death (5-6),
e. This covenant is confirmed to Noah, all mankind, and every living creature on the face of the earth (9-10)
f. The promise is given never to destroy the earth again by a universal flood (11). The next time God destroys the earth, it will be by fire (page, 1456 - 2Pet. 3:10)
g. The rainbow is designated as a testimony to the existence of this covenant and the promise never to destroy the earth by flood. As long as we can see the rainbow, we will know that the Noahic Covenant is in existence (12-17). Now turn to page 18 - Gen. 12:1-3.

The Abrahamic Covenant

Gen. 12:1-3 - The Covenant with Abraham is the first of the theocratic covenants (pertaining to the rule of God). It is unconditional, depending solely upon god who obligates Himself in grace, indicated by the unconditional declaration, I will, to bring to pass the promised blessings. The Abrahamic Covenant is the basis of all the other theocratic covenants and provides for blessings in three areas:

    a. National - "I will make you a great nation."

    b. Personal - "I will bless you and make your name great; and so you shall be a blessing, and

    c. Universal - "In you all the families of the earth shall be blessed."

This covenant was first given in broad outline and was later confirmed to Abraham in greater detail (cf, page, 20 - Gen. 13:14-17; 15:1-7; 18:21; 17:1-8). The Abrahamic Covenant constitutes an important link in all that God began to do, has done throughout history, and will continue to do until the consummation of history. It is the one purpose for humans into which all of God's programs and works fit. The personal aspects of the Abrahamic are four-fold, (1) to be the father of a great nation, (2) to receive personal blessings (3) to receive personal honor and reputation, and (4) to be the source of blessing to others. The universal aspects of the covenant are threefold, (1) blessings for those people and nations which bless Abraham and the nation which comes from him, (2) curses upon those people and nations which curse Abraham and Israel, and (3) blessings upon all the families of the earth through the Messiah, who, according to the flesh, is Abraham's son and provides salvation for the entire world. Now turn to page, 87 - Ex. 19:5-8 - The Mosaic Covenant.

Covenant

One of the most mysterious and yet theologically significant event is recorded in Genesis 15, "In a vision, God told Abram to take a heifer, a goat, a ram, a turtledove, and a young pigeon, and cut all except the birds in half. Then, he was told to place each piece opposite the other."

"Now when the sun was going down, a deep sleep fell upon Abram; and behold terror and great darkness fell upon him." (12) Then God predicted the 400 year bondage of Abram's descendants in a foreign land and their return to Canaan at the end of four generations.

"And it came about, when the sun had set, that it was very dark, and behold there appeared a smoking oven and a flaming torch which passed between these pieces. On the day the Lord made (Heb. Berit) with Abram." (17-18). Then followed the prediction of the extent of the land to be given to Abram's descendants.

The Hebrew idiom "cutting a covenant" was based on the custom of cutting up an animal, and those who were making the covenant walked between the pieces. In this case, only God (visualized as "a smoking oven and a flaming torch") went through. This suggests to many that it was an unconditional covenant on God's part, no matter what Abram did or did not do. Covenant is a word with many shades of meaning, being used for all sorts of formal agreements between people, or between God and men.

The Mosaic Covenant - The covenant with Moses is the second of the theocratic covenants. It is conditional, it is introduced by the conditional formula. "If you will indeed obey My voice, then you shall be My own possession." This covenant was given to the nation of Israel so that those who believed God's promise given to Abraham in the Abrahamic Covenant (Page 18 - Gen. 12:1-3) would know they should conduct themselves. The Mosaic Covenant in its entirety governs three areas of their lives. (1) the commandments governed their personal lives, particularly as they related to God. (Page 88 - Ex. 20:1-26) (2) the judgments governed their social lives particularly as they related to one another (Page 89 - Ex. 21:1 and 24:11) and (3) the ordinances governed their religious lives so that people would know how to approach God on the terms that He dictates (Page 93 - Ex. 24:12 and 31:18). The Mosaic Covenant in no way replaced or set aside the Abrahamic Covenant. Its function is clearly set forth by Paul (Page 1347 Gal. 3:17-19), who points out the law, the Mosaic Covenant, came 430 years after the Abrahamic Covenant. The Mosaic Covenant was added alongside the Abrahamic so that the people of Israel would know how to conduct their lives until the seed, the Christ, comes and makes the complete and perfect sacrifice, toward which the sacrifices of the Mosaic Covenant only point. The Mosaic Covenant was never given so that by keeping it, people could be saved, but so that they might realize that they cannot do what God wants them to do, even when God writes it down on tablets of stone. The law was given that man might realize that he is helpless and hopeless when left to himself, and realize that his only hope is to receive the righteousness of God by faith in Jesus. (Page 1347 - Gal. 3:22-24).

The New Covenant

Jer. 31:31-34 - The new covenant is the fifth and the last of the theocratic covenants (pertaining to the rule of God.) Four provisions are made in this covenant: (a) regeneration - God will put His law in their inward parts and write it in their hearts (31-33) (b) a national restoration - Yahweh will be their God and the nation will be His people, (31-33) (c) personal ministry of the Holy Spirit - they will all be taught individually by God, (31-34) and (d) full justification - their sins will be forgiven and completely removed, (31-34). The New Covenant is made sure by the blood that Jesus shed on Calvary's cross. That blood which guarantees to Israel its New Covenant also provides for the forgiveness of sins for the believers who comprise the Church. Jesus payment for sins is more than adequate to pay for the sins of all who will believe in Him. The New Covenant is called new, in contrast to the covenant with Moses, which is called old. (Page, 850 - Jer. 31:32, page 1423 - Heb. 8:6-13) because it actually accomplishes what the Mosaic Covenant could only point to, that is, the child of God living in a manner that is consistent with the character of God.

Sadly, Israel did not meet the condition of obedience, and is still experienced God's curses and punishment for their disobedience (Page, 232 - Deu. 28:15 and 6:8). God said in Jer. 31:31 "Behold, days are coming, declares the Lord, when I will make a New Covenant with the house of Isreal." Heb. 8-7 "For if that first covenant had been faultless, there would have been no occasion sought for a second." Heb.7:28 "For under the old system, even the High Priests were weak and sinful men who could not keep from doing wrong." Heb. 7:19. "For the law made nothing perfect."

"But later God appointed by His oath His son who is perfect forever." Heb. 7:19. "For the law made nothing perfect, and on the other hand there is a bringing in of a better hope, through which we draw near to God." Heb:10:11. "And every priest stands daily ministering and offering time after time the same sacrifices, which can never take away sins." Heb. 8:3 "For every High Priest is appointed to offer both gifts and sacrifices, hence it is necessary that this High Priest also have something to offer."

Jesus fulfilled these prophecies as Prophet, Priest, and King, but He came to deliver human kind from the reign of sin and bind us into God's family (Luke 4:18-19; Acts 2:36-42) "My Kingdom is not of this world." (John 18:36), He told Pilate. He ruled by serving (Matt. 20:25-28.) As Priest, He offered not the blood of animals but Himself, as full and final sacrifice for sin (John 10:11-18; Heb. 9:12.) Christ is better than the angels, for they worship Him. He is better than Moses, for He created him. He is better than the Aaron priesthood, for His sacrifice was once and for all time. He is better than the Law, for he mediated a better covenant. Christ is our eternal High Priest according to the order of Melchizedek. Since then, we have a great High Priest who has passed through the heavens. (This Jesus is the Son of God, let us hold fast our confession.) For we do not have a High Priest who cannot sympathize with our weaknesses, Christ was not a Levite, but He qualified for a Higher Priesthood according to the order of Melchizedek. The Son of God partook of flesh and blood and was made like His brethren in all things, in order to bring many sons to glory. Christ has become a permanent and perfect High Priest and the mediator of a better covenant. The new covenant has made the old covenant obsolete. He offered Himself as a sinless and voluntary sacrifice, once and for all.

The Temple

The inner room, or holy or holies where the mercy seat was, the high priest went into once a year. Christ's superiority to the temple was clearly shown when the veil of the temple was split from top to bottom at His death. (Matt. 27:51) The veil hung before the most sacred place in the temple to keep out all person except the Jewish high priest. God's presence was manifested in the Most Holy Place as a cloud. (1Kings 8:5-11). The tearing of the veil symbolized that every believer has unhindered access to God through His Son Jesus Christ because of His sacrificial death on our behalf. Heb. 9:12 - And not through the blood of goats and calves, but through His own blood. He entered the

154

Holy place once and for all, having obtained eternal redemption. He offered one sacrifice for sins for all time, sat down at the right hand of God. Rom. 10:4 - says Christ is the end of the law. It was evident that our Lord was descended from Judah, a tribe with reference to which Moses spoke nothing concerning priests. But God called the Levis to the priesthood, in Heb. 7:5 - Christ was not a Levi, but He became High Priest through the tribe of Judah, Gal. 2:16.

The New Covenant

1 Cor. 11:25 "This is the New Covenant. This is the New Covenant in My blood, do this, as often as you drink it, in remembrance of Me." Rom. 11:27 "And this is My Covenant with them. When I take away their sins." Jer. 31:33 "But this is the Covenant which I will make with the house of Israel after those days, declares the Lord, I will put My law within them, and on their hearts. I will write it and I will be their God, and they shall be My people." Heb. 10:1 "I will put My laws into their minds, and I will write them upon their hearts." Luke 22:20 "And in the same way He took the cup after they had eaten, saying, This cup which is poured out for you is the New Covenant in My blood." 2Cor 3:6 "Who also made us adequate as servants of a New Covenant, not of the letter, but of the Spirit for the letter kills, but the Spirit gives life. This is My New Covenant." Matt. 26:28 "For this is My blood of the Covenant which is poured out for many for forgiveness of sin." Acts 10:43 "Of Him all the prophets bear witness that through His name everyone who believes in Him received forgiveness of sins." Mark 14:24 "And He said to them, This is My blood of the Covenant, which is poured our for many." 1 Cor. 11:24-25 "This is My body, which is for you, do this as often as you drink it in remembrance of Me." Acts 13:39 "And through Him everyone who believes

is freed from all things, from which you could not be freed through the Law of Moses." Rom. 7:6 "But now we have been released from the Law, having died to that by which we were bound, so that we serve in newness of the Spirit and not in oldness of the letter." Rom. 10:4 "For Christ is the end of the Law for righteousness to everyone who believes, (5) For Moses writes that the man who practices the righteousness which is based on the law shall live by that righteousness. (6) But the righteousness based on faith speaks thus, Do not say in your hearts who will ascend into Heaven?" Rom. 7:4 "Therefore my brethren, you also were made to die to the Law through the body of Christ, that you might be joined to another, to Him who was raised from the dead, that we might bear fruit for God." Gal. 2:16 "Nevertheless knowing that a man is not justified by the works of the law but through faith in Christ Jesus, even we have believed in Christ Jesus, that we may be justified by faith in Christ, and not by the works of the Law, since the works of the Law shall no flesh be justified." Gal. 15:4 "You have been severed from Christ, you who are seeking to be justified by law, you have fallen from grace." Gal. 12:19 "For through the Law I died to the Law, that I might live to God."

Christ's Eternal Priesthood

Chapter 7:11-12, Levitical Priesthood was Temporary

Those earlier sacrifices were imperfect and insufficient to take away Sins (Heb. 10:4). It was Carnal (16), that is, they were Priests solely because they were of a certain family, without regard to spiritual qualifications. And the Covenant under which they operated has been superseded by another covenant. Under the old Covenant were God's statutes and ordinances, and His commandments governing their live and tithes.

Chapter 7:13-28, Christ's Eternal Priesthood

Levitical Priests offered sacrifices every year, Christ died once and for all. Their sacrifices were unavailing, removed sin forever. Christ lives on, mediator of an Eternal Covenant and Endless Life. Eternal is one of the favorite words of the Epistles. Eternal Salvation (5-9), Eternal Judgment (6-2), Eternal Redemption (9-12), Eternal Spirit (9-14), Eternal Inheritance (9-15), Eternal Covenant (13-20). It is also a favorite word in John's gospel.

Chapter 8 - The New Covenant

Christ brought to mankind a New Covenant. The First Covenant, centered around the Tabernacle Services and the Ten Commandments, had served its purpose (9-1-5). Its Laws were written on tablets of stone (9-4). Christ's Laws would be written on our Hearts (8-10). The First Covenant was Temporal, Christ's Covenant would be Everlasting (13-20). The First Covenant was sealed with the blood of animals; Christ Covenant was sealed with His Own Blood (10-29), it was a better Covenant, with better promises, based on the Immutability of God's Word, (6-18).

The New Covenant is here called The New Testament. A testament is "a Will, a bequeath to heirs, effective only after the death of the maker." The New Covenant is the Will which Christ made for His Heirs, which could not become effective till, by His Death, He had atoned for their sins.

This is where we get the names of the Two Divisions of the Bible; Old Testament and New Testament. The New Testament is the story of the Covenant of Christ. The abundant use of Blood in the rites of the Old Covenant prefigured the urgent necessity of some Great Sacrifice for Human Sin (19-22)

Once and for all (26-28), Christ offered Himself. Once and for all, He entered the Holy Place (9-12). Once and for all He put away sin at the end of the ages (9-26). (Men appointed once to die) (9-27). Christians sanctified once and for all by the offering of Christ (10-10), Christ once offered shall appear a second time for His waiting heirs (9-28). Here the Lord's coming again is called His second coming.

(Chapter 10:1-25 Sin Removed Forever)

No need for further sacrifice, Christ's Death is entirely sufficient to take care of all previous sin, and those that in weakness we may in daily life commit, God can now Forgive, and will Forgive, those who place their Truth in Christ.

"Let us therefore hold fast to Christ." (23) "He alone, is our Home and our Savior." -

The Law and the Gospel

We are introduced to the Levitical Law in the early history of the children of Israel. As Israel had now become a nation and was soon to be in possession of the land of promise, it was fitting that the nation of God's people should have a written law of God to govern them. This law was given at Sinai, (Ex. 19). It was in force until the institution of the Gospel of Christ, Matt. 5:17-20; John 1:17; Col. 2:6-17. -

What the Levitical Law was under the Old Dispensation, the Gospel of Christ is under the New - the supreme law of God for the people of God under their respective dispensations. There is perfect harmony and unity between these two. Yet, they are essentially different in a number of respects.

Does God change? "No, I change not." (Mal. 3:6), is His answer to this question. Does His law change? Yes and no. The principles of everlasting truth are as firmly established under the Law as under the Gospel - the Word of God is the same in both. But God, like every wise administrator, changes the application of His laws to fit existing conditions from time to time. To illustrate; a son comes to the father one day and says, "Father, may I go to town?" "No," says the father. The next day the son comes again and says, "Father, may I go to town?" "Yes," says the father. Has the father changed? No; but the conditions have changed, and this makes it proper for the son to go today though it would have been improper yesterday. In like manner has God inserted some things in the New Covenant which are "not according" to corresponding things in the Old, not because He has changed or that truth has changed; but because of changed conditions. He applies eternal truths to existing conditions in the present dispensation. On this point I submit the following comparisons for consideration.

To rightly divide the Word of Truth it is necessary to kee in mind the following:

1. That God has given two distinct covenants, the Old and New Testaments. (Heb. 8:6-10).

2. That in the light of changed conditions, God in His wisdom saw fit to forbid in the New some things that were commanded in the Old. (Matt. 5:38-39; Ex. 21:23-25; Jer. 31:31-32; Heb. 7:12)

3. That the Old Testament was the rule of life to Israel up to the time of Christ's death on the cross. (Gal. 3:23-25; Col. 2:14; Eph 2:14-15).

3. That the New Testament is now the rule for Christian conduct until Christ comes. (1 Cor. 3:6-11; 1Thess. 1:7-8),

4. That the Christian has the Old Testament as a mine of rich

instruction, essential to the proper understanding of the New. (1 Cor. 10: 6-11; Gal. 3:24-25)

5. That the Old was taken away that the New might be established as our only rule of life (Heb.10:9-10; Gal. 1:8 9)

6. That those who persist in substituting Old Testament doctrine for New Testament teaching subvert the souls o their hearers. (Acts 15:24; Tit. 1:9-11)

Two Spokesmen

Both Old and New dispensations are provided with a spokesman, a mediator, a prophet, a lawgiver, one authorized by Almighty god to speak for his own dispensation - Moses under the Old, Jesus Christ under the New. It was concerning Jesus of Nazareth that Moses spoke, saying, "A prophet shall the Lord your God raise up unto you of your brethren, like unto me; him shall ye hear." (Acts 7:37) An additional though is given in Heb. 1:1-2. "God, who at sundry times and in divers manners spake in time past unto the father by the prophets, hath in these last days spoken unto us by His son." The Father speaking from heaven puts emphasis on the thought of Christ's being the authorized spokesman for this dispensation when He says (Matt. 17:5) "This is My beloved Son, in whom I am well pleased; hear ye Him." Let us again quote from Heb. 12:25, "See that ye refuse not him that speaketh, For if they escaped not who refused him that spake on earth, much more shall not we escape if we turn away from Him that speaketh from heaven."

The thought conveyed in the last scripture quoted makes it clear that while in the Old Dispensation they looked to the law of Moses (which tithings and offerings were under) for their rule of life. In our times we look to the Gospel as our supreme law. (This thought will be developed later.)

Two Covenants

Paul, in comparing these covenants, says, "But now hat he obtained a more excellent ministry, by how much also He is mediator of a better covenant which was established upon better promise." (For if that first covenant had been faultless.) The first covenant was under the Mosaic Law, of God's statutes and ordinances, which tithes were under, and offerings were offered to God for their sins. These offerings came from tithes, Num. 18:26. These offerings didn't take away sins. They only covered their sin. The people of the nations of Israel turned from God to other gods, stopped tithing, and offering sacrifice to God for their sins, then should no place have been sought for the second covenant. For finding fault with them. He said, "Behold, the days come, said the Lord, when I will make a New Covenant with the house of Israel and with the house of Judah. (Heb. 8:6-8)

Two very remarkable expressions, among other things, are found in this scripture; more excellent ministry, "better covenant." The first refers to Christ and His work, as compared with Moses and the work of the Levitical priesthood. The conclusion is natural, and accepted with little difficulty. But what are we to say with reference to the "Better Covenant?" Was the old one faulty?

By no means, the law is holy, and the commandments holy and "are just, and good." Rom. 7:12. There is absolutely no flaw, no imperfection in the law of God. The law of Moses, like the Gospel of Christ, is the law of God. It was conceived in the mind of God, and is therefore perfect, absolutely perfect. But it was weak through the flesh (Rom. 8:3); or in other words, it required absolute perfection on the part of the individual before any individual could be justified by it. Therefore by the

161

law can no flesh be justified.

Law and Grace

Paul wrote to the Galatians, saying, "The law was our schoolmaster to bring us unto Christ." (Gal. 3:24). It was right in its place, in its time, for its purpose, pure, just, holy, righteous, perfect. It served its purpose, was fulfilled in Christ, nailed to the cross. The Mosaic law was God's statutes, and ordinances and His commandments, that tithes, and offering were under. (Col. 2:14). So, we were heathen at that time, without God in the world. Israel was God's chosen people, all other nations served other gods. (Col. 2:14). So we today are not under the law, but under the Gospel of Christ. We look to Him as our Savior and Redeemer, our Lawgiver and Supreme Authority, and we no longer look to the ceremonial law, which was under the law and nailed to the cross by our Lord Jesus Christ. No longer do we look to the ceremonial laws to find what is the will of the Lord concerning us for our times, but rather to the Gospel of Christ. For this reason, therefore, the covenant of grace is the better covenant as compared to the covenant of law.

John gives voice to a significant thought when he says, "The law was given by Moses, but grace and truth came by Jesus Christ." (John 1:17). One symbolizes the justice and power of God, the other His mercy and grace. Under the first covenant the seal was by the blood of animal; under the second, the blood of Jesus Christ, "slain from the foundation of the World." (Rev. 13:8). ⬅

One of the marked distinctions between the Law and the Gospel is the manner of dealing with transgressors. That was a dispensation of justice, as evident from the number that perished during the wilderness journey from Egypt to Canaan, from the stoning of Achan, the smiting of Uzzah (1 Sam. 6:6-7), the judgment of God upon Israel and Judah for their unfaithfulness, etc. Ours is a dispensation of mercy, as evident from God's mercy in the midst of wickedness on the part of people bearing His name, and the sacrifices of the Lamb of God that all the world may go free. But let not man get the idea that God will deal more leniently with His people of this dispensation that He did with the people in former times. In that day the looked forward by faith (Heb. 11), and though dying without realization of the promise in their day. God's dealing with His people in that day were intended as an example to us. (1 Cor. 10:6-11). To the end that the grace of God may not have been bestowed upon us in vain, emphatic warning is given us that they who spurn God's grace in time must suffer His wrath in eternity. (1 Thess. 1:7-9; Heb. 12:25).

The Law and the Gospel are interdependent. All the sacrifices, offerings and the ceremonies under the Law were but typical of Christ, and would have amounted to nothing but for their fulfillment in Christ who by one offering perfected forever those that are sanctified. (Heb. 10:14). On the other hand, "the law was our schoolmaster to bring us to Christ," and today the Gospel means more to us because of the light shed upon it by the message of the Law and because of the type, means, image, and shadows found in the Old Testament. Nevertheless, when it comes to the law now in force, we find it in the Gospel. That is now the discipline by which the Christian Church is governed, the Word of God by which our destiny is determined.

Centered in the Law are the thirty-nine messages or books of the Old Testament. Centered in the Gospel are the twenty-seven messages or books of the New Testament. The whole constitutes a perfect message from God to man, the sacred canon of the Holy Scriptures, the Book which we have learned to cherish one which we call the Bible.

Leviticus 5:1-10, Christ Compared to Levitical Priests

They were of the Tribe of Levi; Christ was of the Tribe of Judah. They were many. He was One. They offered animal sacrifices; he offered Himself. They died; He lives.

The point is that there has been One Sacrifice for Sin. There will never be another, whoever will not avail himself of what Christ has done for him on the Cross may as well make up his mind to say good-bye to God forever, and go his way, and suffer for his own sins.

The Levites were divinely ordained as mediators between God and the Hebrew nation in the ministry of animal sacrifices. Those sacrifices were fulfilled in Christ. Animal sacrifices are no longer necessary. Christ Himself is the Great High Priest for man; the Only mediator between God and man. Hebrews 8:9-10, makes this very clear.

The Epistle to the Hebrews was written to show that Priests were no longer necessary.

Reconciliation of Jews and Gentiles

Here is when we Gentiles came to God. (Eph 2:11-22) Eph 2:11 "Therefore remember, that formerly you, (the Gentiles) were in the flesh, who are called Uncircumcised by the so-called 'Circumcision,' which is performed on the flesh by human hands." (

Eph. 2:12 "Remember that you were at that time separate from Christ, excluded from the commonwealth of Israel, and strangers to covenants of promise, having no hope and without God in the world.".

Eph. 2:13 "But now in Christ Jesus you who formerly were far off have been brought near by the blood of Christ."

Eph. 2:14 "For He Himself is our peace who made both

groups into one, and broke down the barrier of the dividing wall."

Eph. 2:15 "By abolishing in His flesh the enmity which is the Law of commandments contained in ordinances, that in Himself He might make the two into one new man, thus establishing peace."

Eph. 2:16 "And might reconcile them both in one body to God through the cross by it having put to death the enmity."

Eph. 2:17 "And He came and preached peace to you who were far away, and peace to those who were near."

Eph. 2:18 "For through Him we both have our access in one Spirit to the Father."

Eph. 2:19 "So then you are no longer strangers and aliens, but you are fellow citizens with the saints, and are of God's household.

This is who god sent to the Gentiles.

Acts 9:15 "But the Lord said to him, Go for he is a chosen instrument of Mine, to bear My name before the Gentiles and Kings and the sons of Israel."

(24) "Therefore the Law has become our tutor to lead us to Christ, that we may be justified by faith."

God chose Saul to go and bear His name before the Gentiles.

Acts 2:21 "And it shall be, that everyone who calls on the name of the Lord shall be saved."

Acts 10:45 "And all the circumcised believers who had come with Peter were amaze, because the gift of the Holy Spirit had been poured upon the Gentiles also, (46) For they were hearing them speaking with tongues and exalting God."

Acts 11:1 "Now the apostles and the brethren who were throughout Judea heard that the Gentiles also had received the word of God."

Acts 13:46-48 "And Paul and Barnabas spoke out boldly and said, It was necessary that the word of God should be spoken to you first; since you repudiate it, and judge yourselves unworthy of eternal life, behold, we are turning to the Gentiles."

Acts 13:47 "I have placed you as a light for the Gentiles, that you should bring salvation to the end of the Earth. (48) And when the Gentiles heard this, they began rejoicing and glorifying the word of the Lord; and many as had been appointed to eternal life believed."

Acts 18:6 "And when they resisted and blasphemed, he shook out his garments and said to them, Your blood be upon your own heads. I am clean. From now on I shall go to the Gentiles."

When studying the Bible always find out how words are used, and what generation He is speaking to. Then, you will find out the truth.

Chapter 12

This message is for you, Pastor, knowing God's word about what tithes are, but not honoring or respecting His word about tithes not being money, you have turned to your own righteousness to lie about tithes being money.

To God be the glory for His sustaining grace while this word was in the course of preparation. In all that I endeavored to write about, I took it as a matter of course that a plain "thus said the Lord" is the final word on any subject under consideration about what tithes are. I have tried to cover the entire range of the scripture on tithes, though limited space compelled me to be true of this subject. I would like to have considered at greater length, and the reader will no doubt find all truths that will enrich their thoughts found in this book that might have been very materially improved and strengthened.

While the entire message is intended as an exposition of Christian doctrine on the truth about tithes, and offerings, my aim is to reach the hearts of Christians as well as their heads, to appeal to the conscience as well as their understanding as to what tithes are, to make this message practical as well as exegetical. How well we succeeded or failed, by lying and saying that we should tithe, I will let you be your own judge on your own righteousness or on your unrighteousness about tithes, Pastor. You are your own judge, Pastor.

Another thing that should be mentioned is that, whatever the point under discussion, my aim was to quote just enough scripture to make the point clear and convincing, rather than to attempt to quote all scripture bearing on said point. I endeavored to make the message brief. This message is intended for you, Pastor. The burden of this message is to uphold our Lord's Holy Word, His infallible Word, to magnify the Word of the Lord, and to endear the message of the Cross to the hearts of the readers. With a prayer that the blessing of the Lord may be added to the imperfect efforts put forth and that the entire body of readers may together support the full truths of the Gospel. I submit this message for your consideration, that Christ Jesus fulfilled the Law which tithes and offerings were under, in Heb. 8:13 and also in Rom. 10:4 - is the end of the Law that tithes were under, we are now under a new Covenant, the blood of Christ, Matt. 26:28.

Pastor, Blessed is he that keepeth the saying and the truth of the Bible. The sayings of the Bible are doctrines of our Lord, and clearly God's Inspired Infallible Word. To keep these truths is to be divinely blessed. The right keeping of the teachings of the Word of God necessarily depend on the right understanding of the truth about God's word. Pastor, rightly divide the word of truth about tithes, it is necessary to keep in mind the following, Christian doctrine involves the commandments, teachings, standards, and principles essential to saving faith and victorious life.

Pastor, if tithes are money, then God made a great mistake, or our Pastors are lying about tithes being money. Pastor, God is not the author of confusion. The word of God and the spirit of God agree in all things concerning His word, for He cannot be a true God and contradict Himself. He cannot say the Law is over in Heb. 8:13 and Rom. 10:4, then say for us to pay tithes. It would be so confusing for us to pay tithes, and then say in Luke,

6:38 "Give and it shall be given to you," and in Acts 20:35 "It is more blessed to give than to receive." In 2 Cor. 9:6-7 "He which soweth sparingly shall reap also sparingly. Let every man give according as he purposeth in his heart." It would be very confusing to say tithe, then put scriptures saying other things about giving. Pastor, the word of God and spirit of God agree in all things concerning His word, for He cannot be a true God and contradict Himself. The word of God is absolutely trustworthy and reliable. It is infallible, it is the inspired word of God. Pastor, what it says about tithes cannot be changed by you, Pastor.

No sooner had God placed man upon the earth and surrounded him with the beauty and inspiration of the universe then He presented a series of teachings involving the principles that make for a successful life. The keeping of the Word of God is your victory or defeat, conditioned upon your accepting or rejecting the Word as true, as the doctrines of God laid down by divine authority, which is God's Holy Inspired Infallible Word.

When Jesus, the Great Teacher, concluded His discourse in which He set forth the vital requirements for a life acceptable in His sight, He declared that the successful career depended upon hearing and doing His saying. The Holy Spirit is instructing the leaders of the Christian Church constantly to the fact that in order to meet the approval of the Shepherd and Bishop of our souls it is essential to live, teach, and instill in the lives of His followers the doctrines of the Word of God. 1 Tim. 16:17 - We are taught that all teachings of the Word of God are essential in fully equipping the Christian work. To teach us that tithes are for us and that tithes are money and is God's doctrines for us today, is wicked, immoral, and misleading. Again, in 1 Tim. 4:16 - We have this very direct teaching "Take heed unto thyself and unto the true doctrines of God and His word about what tithes are: continue in the truths about tithes, for in doing this thou shall honor His word, God will be pleased with you in this."

In this critical age of liberal and modern tendencies and positions, that characterize so many present day theologians and institutions of learning, it is very essential indeed that the Church Pastor have a work of vital doctrine that rings clear, and is free from the blasting influence of false teachings. Teaching tithing in the Church is a false doctrine. It is unrighteousness on your part, Pastor, to teach tithing for us today. It is highly necessary that Christians know what are the true teachings of the Inspired Word, and that they make true doctrine on tithes a part of our faith, and life. It makes a difference that we believe the truth about God's Word on tithes. It makes a difference as to what is our attitude toward the full truth of God's inspirational Word on tithes and all truths of His Holy Word. It is necessary to set all Christians free from the Curse of the Law.

It makes a difference as to what we think of the Sonship of Christ. His virgin birth, His vicarious suffering, His atonement for sin, His bodily resurrection, His victorious ascension, His place at the right hand of the Father, His glorious coming again, the judgments He will measure out to the disobedient, and the eternal rewards He will give to the faithful, Pastor. This book, carefully studied and its teaching fully practiced, must bring into the life of the individual a true attitude toward God's Word about tithes. In view of these terrible facts and in the light of the Knowledge we have of the eternal Word, and with a consciousness of the tremendous responsibility resting upon Pastor, with is his only mission it is to lead men into the glorious light on tithes.

God is not an autocrat who decides the destinies of men according to an arbitrary will. He governs in mercy and righteousness through laws founded upon the principles of everlasting truth and justice, and all will be judged according to the law and evidence. What we call "the Laws of nature" are but the laws of God, conceived in His infinite wisdom and love and put into operation by His mighty power. By these of God we are governed here, and will be judged hereafter. As Jesus puts it, "The word that I have spoken, the same shall judge him in the last day." (John 12:48). Exact and perfect justice and mercy are possible because God has fixed laws, impartially administered; "for God is no respecter of person." (Acts 10:34) The joys and sorrows of life are experienced as God's laws are obeyed or violated, for "whatsoever a man soweth that shall he also reap." Pastor, (Gal. 6:7) "He hath appointed a day, in which He will judge the world in righteousness by that man whom He hath ordained."

Pastor, God is inspired, infinite in wisdom, knowledge, and soundness of judgment. He is unchangeable, and therefore thoroughly righteous and reliable. We may express opinions, may differ from other people in view of religion or duty, but we are very thankful that the matter of deciding upon what shall their lot in eternity is reserved for Him whose knowledge is infinite and whose judgment is perfect. It is wrong for you, Pastor, to express your opinion on any subject upon which the scripture light shines. He is perfect in righteousness, so we may expect nothing, but simple justice. He is impartial, and therefore no respecter of persons. This is the character of the great judge before whom we all shall stand - and if in this life we are wise and judge ourselves according to His standard of everlasting truth and righteousness while this opportunity is still ours, we are assured that our judgment at that great day will be commendation rather than the sentence of eternal death because of our sins.

It may be well to add that no other being, besides the Divine Judge, is qualified to serve in that capacity. Here, as in all other cases, God has manifested His wisdom and grace in the provisions made for our well-being.

The Judgment

1. It will be according to the law and the evidence.

Christ makes it clear that He is not an arbitrary judge, but that His mission in the World was to save men, not to condemn them (John 3:17; 12:47); and that when He comes the second time it will be with the same heart of love, as the Friend to humanity, meting out justice according to the Word (John 12:48) and according to our works (2 Cor. 5:10). As a man in court is brought before a bar of justice to be justified or sentenced according to the law and the evidence, so will our standing before the great Judge depend upon how our record compares with the eternal Word of God. The law being established forever (Psa. 119:89), "the only point to be decided is as to whether our record here has been such as to establish our innocence or guilt before the law. If we would judge ourselves, we should not be judged." (1 Cor. 11:31). If we accepted God's grace in Jesus Christ, we shall then stand justified in the record if not, we shall remain condemned. All this will appear in the evidence. Here, not yonder, is where our eternal fate is determined. However merciful a judge may be, justice demands that all who are brought before Him declared innocent or guilty, depending upon the law and the evidence. The law being established forever, and our record established at the time of our death, there remains nothing to do for the great Judge but to assign us to the place where our records, according to the law and the evidence, prove us to belong. Matt. 25:41.

"God spared not the angels that sinned, but cast them down to hell, to be reserved unto judgment." (2 Peter 2:4). Jude also testifies that the angels which kept not their first estate, but left their own habitation, he hath reserved in everlasting chains under darkness unto the judgment of the great day. In the end, the fallen angels will share the same fate as fallen men - both will be sent "into everlasting fire, prepared for the devil and his angel." Matt. 25:41.

The wicked shall be turned into hell, "Choosing the path of sin in this world, they will reap the fruits of their unrighteousness in the world to come (Matt 7:13; Rom. 1:18, 32:6-23; Jude 8:16).

How God Describes Heaven

To those who expect to spend eternity in heaven the commandment is, "Be ye holy; for I am holy." (1 Pet. 1:16). The angels of God are spoken of as "holy angels." (Matt. 25:31). Nothing unholy will ever be permitted, "there shall in no wise enter into it anything that defileth, neither whatsoever worketh abomination, or maketh a lie; but they which are written in the Lamb's book of life." (Rev. 21:27). Without peace and holiness, "no man shall see the Lord." (Heb. 12:14). Holy, thrice holy, forever holy is the eternal dwelling place of God.

The "heaven of heavens" the place where God dwells, the eternal "paradise of God," where God and saints and angels will spend eternity.

1. (John 14:1-3), Christ comforted His disciples, saying, "I go to prepare a place for you, And if I go and prepare a place for you, I will come again, and receive you unto Myself." From this and similar scripture we understand that heaven is not merely a condition but a place, the eternal dwelling place of God, where God the Savior dwells, and where saints and angels will spend eternity with Him.

2. "It is a high and holy place." (Isa. 57:15). This gives us the added thought that of all places heaven is "the high and holy" place - high, because it is above all other places; holy,

173

because it is inhabited by holy beings only, and sin will never enter there. The seraphim sang, "holy, holy, holy, is the Lord of Host," (Isa. 6:3), and worshipers in glory will continue to take up this sweet refrain. The holy of holies, in the tabernacle in the wilderness, and later in the temple, typified heaven. (Heb. (:1-12)

How to Manifest Our Love to God

We can manifest our love to God by an obedient life. Christ sounded the keynote when He said, "If ye love Me; keep My commandments." Again, He puts the same truth in different form when He says, "Ye are My friends, if ye do whatsoever I command you." (John 15:14). Again, in the same discourse, "He that hath My commandments, and keepeth them, he it is that loveth Me. (John 14:21). In verse 23, He says, "If a man love Me, he will keep My words." Pastor, God's word on tithes is not for us, you have tried to change tithes to money. That's nothing but a fable. God's word about tithes lasts throughout eternity. God is saying to all Pastors that His word is Immutable and if you love Him keep the truth. Love and obedience are inseparable. You never saw a man whose love for God was greater than his love for the World but that he made it an invariable practice to "obey God rather than men."

"The Father hath committed all judgment unto the Son. That all man should honor the Son even as they honor the Father."

Pastor, Benny Hinn, Pastor, John Hagee, Pastor Creflo Dollar, Pastor, Jesse Duplantis, Bishop, Clarence McZenod, Pastor Mac Hammond, Pastor Chris LeGrande, Pastor, R.W. Schamback, Pastor Rod Parsley, Pastor Kenneth Copeland, Bishop Charles Blake, Bishop Gilbert E. Patterson.

I am not trying to judge you, Pastor, or bring any charges against God's elect. As the bible says, don't bring any charges against God's elect. My purpose is to ask you, Pastor, and all Pastors that are receiving tithes from their members, WHY are you Pastors asking your members for tithes in this generation? Christ did away with the law tithing was under. Pastors that are still asking your members for tithes, have an obligation to be faithful and loyal to God's word and faithful to one's oath to God to teach and preach the truth of His word about tithes.

It is the Spirit of God that guides into all truth. (John 16:13). No man truthfully claims obedience to God without submission to the wooings and leadings of the Holy Spirit. It is impossible to separate God from His Word. The power of God being in His Word, we understand what Paul meant when he declared the Gospel of Christ to be "the power of God unto salvation." (Rom. 1:16). It is idle to thing of being right with God without being obedient to His Word (John 14:15, 15:14; Jas. 1:22-25; 1John 2:3-4). As the Word of God is the message of God to man, so the Church of God is the organization through which this message is brought to a lost world. (Matt. 28:18-20.) Lie not to one another, Pastor as about tithing. Every form of untruth and dishonesty comes from the "father of lies." (John 8:44)

The Unspotted Life

This is the "pure religion" of which James speaks, undefiled before God, and to keep himself unspotted from the World. (Jas.1:27) this includes purity of thought, of life, of speech, of every Christian virtue, freedom from every form of ungodliness. "Blessed are the pure in heart; for they shall see God." (Matt. 5:8)

Pastor, God said in 2 Tim 3:16 "All scripture is given by inspiration of God, and is profitable for doctrine, for reproof, for correction, for instruction in righteousness."

Pastor, God is saying in 2 Tim 3:16 - All scripture is given by inspiration of God. All, means every one of the scriptures, the books of the Old and New Testament.

2 Tim 3:17 "That the man of God may be perfect, thoroughly furnished unto all good words." Living Bible. It is God's way of making us well prepared at every point, fully equipped to do good to everyone.

Tim. 4:2 - God is saying to all Pastors to "preach the word, be instant in season, out of season, reprove, rebuke, exhort with all long-suffering and doctrine."

Living Bible 2Tim. 4:2 "To preach the word of God urgently at all times, whenever you get the chance, in season and out, when it is convenient and when it is not. Correct and rebuke your people when they need it, encourage them to do right, and all the time be feeding them patiently with God's Word."

2 Tim. 4:2 - God is saying to all Pastors to preach the word. His inspired word, which is infallible.

Pastor, god said in 2 Tim. 4:3 "For the time will come when they will not endure sound doctrine."

Dishonesty

Lie not to one another is advice that all people need. 2 Cor. 4:2-4 "Every form of untruth and dishonesty comes from "the father of lies."

Purity

This includes purity of thought, of life, of speech, of every Christian virtue, freedom from every form of ungodliness.

1 Thess. 5:22 - God is saying to us, Pastor, to abstain from all appearance of evil. Keep away from every kind of evil. It is evil to turn God's word into a fable, about tithes.

1 John 5:17 "All unrighteousness is sin; and there is a sin not unto death."

Heb. 4:12 "For the word of God is quick, and powerful, and sharper than any two edged sword, piercing even to the dividing asunder of soul and spirit, and of the joints and marrow, and is a discerner of the thoughts and intents of the heart." Pastor, Pastor, Pastor, don't you know that God said to abstain from all appearances of evil, and to preach His word in season and out of season, and not to preach His word for filthy lucre. Some Pastors have been lying to us too long about God saying for them to take tithes from us in these days. How can you, as a Shepherd over God's flock lie about Him, then say that you are honoring God's word when you're lying about tithes? Pastor, God cannot ask us to give Him tithes, because tithes have never been money. Tithes were used as an offering, as a sacrifice for the sins of the nation of Israel.

How can some Pastors say they are doing the will of God, but lying about Him all the time? This is your self will. Of all the possible sins against God, Pastor, THE most serious is that of self will. This sin led to the fall of Satan (Isa. 14:12-14). And it can be said to be the root of Adam's transgression (Gen. 3:1-7). It is, therefore, of utmost importance that the child of God find His will and perform it, Pastor. The holy spirit will convict the willing heart of its power. All Scripture is inspired by God, wrote the Christian Apostle Paul. (1 Tim. 3:16) But it seems that some Pastors will is to change God's word about tithes, for the love of money. It is not righteousness on your part, Pastor, to do this for the love of money.

The second principle of interpretation is to interpret the Bible in light of its historical background, interpreting the Bible according to all of the parallel passages which deal with the subject, and according to the message of the entire Bible.

The Bible reveals the nature of God as spirit, unity and trinity. He is a spirit — a personal, infinite being (John 4:24). He is one-one in substance or nature and incapable of being divid-

177

ed into separate parts (Deu. 6:4) and He is three eternally existing in three coequal persons (Matt. 28:19). While great mystery surrounds God's nature, it is reassuring to know that God is above us.

Worshipping God is essential, also to spiritual growth. Worshipping, Pastor, involves honor and respect toward God. Word, Pastor, Christians who submit to the Lordship of Christ in reverence and service will grow in their spiritual lives.

Pastor, he that comes to God must believe He is divine, Holy, and that He is spirit, sinless, and that God honors only His Word, that God is true to His Word. We must believe that God is the same, yesterday, today, and forever. They that worship Him must worship Him in spirit and truth. As Christians, we must honor and respect His word about what tithes are.

Pastor, you were called by God to preach His word, apparently Satan has also called. The Devil has blinded your eyes, and minds from the truth of God's word on tithes. He also has taken the truth of God's word on tithes. He also has taken the truth of God's word on tithes from your hearts and the apparently controls your testimony, and devours your mind to resist in deception. 2 Cor. 4:4 "For in whose case the god of this world has blinded the minds of the unbelieving, that they might not see the light of the gospel of the Glory of Christ, who is the image of God." (Luke 8:12) "And those beside the road are those who have heard; them the devil comes and takes away the word from their heart, so that they may not believe and be saved." (Acts 13:8) "But Elymas the magician [for thus his name is translated] was opposing them, seeking to turn the proconsul away from the faith (1 Pet. 5:8) "Be of sober spirit, be on the alert. Your adversary, the devil, prowls about like a roaring lion, seeking someone to devour." (1 Pet. 5:9) "But resist him firm in your faith, knowing that the same experiences of suffering are being accomplished by your brethren who are in the world." (1 Cor.

7:5) "Stop depriving one another, except by agreement for a time that you may devote yourselves to prayer, and come together again lest Satan tempt you because of your lack of self-control." (2 Cor. 2:11) "In order that not advantage be taken of us by Satan; for we are not ignorant of his schemes." (Eph. 6:11) "Put on the full armor of God, that you may be able to stand firm against the schemes of the devil."

Some Pastors are not adhering steadfastly to faith in God's word on what tithes were. Satan has tempted you to immorality. Pastor, God doesn't bless or His blessing is not on filthy-lucre, because the word of God and the Spirit of God agree in all things concerning His word. He cannot be a true God and contradict Himself. Tithes are not money.

Bishop Clarence McZendon, why do you teach that tithes are money? You don't have to falsely teach about tithes being money, because God said in His Holy Inspired Infallible Word, that He would supply all your needs according to is riches in glory by Christ Jesus. And that whatsoever you ask the Father in His name He would give it to you. All Pastors that are teaching tithes have lost faith in god's word, because they don't believe that God will supply all their needs. He said that in Phi. 4:19 and in 1 John 5:15. He said ask anything in My name, the Father will give it you. God said in Heb. 11:6, Bishop Clarence McZendon, "And without faith it is impossible to please Him, for he who comes to God must believe that He is, and that He is a rewarder of those who seek Him." You don't believe that, because you are teaching tithes being money.

Gal. 6:8 "For he that soweth to his flesh shall of the flesh reap corruption; but he that soweth to the Spirit shall of the Spirit reap life everlasting."

Living Bible, "If he sows to pleas his own wrong desires, he will be planting seeds of evil and he will surely reap a harvest of spiritual decay and death; but if he plants the good things of the Spirit, he will reap the everlasting life which the Holy spirit gives him."

Bishop Clarence McZendon, and Bishop Gilbert E. Patterson, and Bishop Charles Blake. This message is for all three of you, you Bishops or Pastors don't have any fear about what God said about adding to His Word. This is adding to His Word when you are teaching tithes in His Church, and that tithes are money. Both Pastors and Bishops are also teaching that Abram gave Melchizedek tithes, yes, he gave them tithes, but it wasn't money.

Bishop Clarence McZendon, you were teaching tithing on Channel 40 about Abram giving Melchizedek tithes, a tenth part and this tenth was money. You also said God opened the windows of heaven and poured out a blessing to him for tithing. Wrong! God said that to the nation of Israel, in Mal. 3:10 - not to Abram. Melchizedek was the one who gave him the blessing in Gen. 14:19. And you were also teaching on TV asking people to send a heaving offering. Everything you taught was false, and deceptive because you know that most people don't read their Bibles and they believe a Pastor won't teach untruth. They don't know God said there would be false teachers like you. Teaching that tithes are money makes you a false teacher.

Bishop Clarence McZendon, how can you be that wicked by lying on TV, asking people to send in a heaving offering of $98,000. This is deceptive, and morally wrong.

Ex. 29:27 "The best part of the ram, the thigh and breast portion was consecrated. The wave offering was consecrated to the Lord by rite of the heave offering.

E. 29:27 - Wave offering, Ref. Smith Bible Dic., page 737 - This rite, together with that of heaving or raising the offering, was an inseparable accompaniment of peace offerings. In such the right shoulder, considered the choicest part of the victim, was to be heaved, and viewed as holy to the Lord, only eaten therefore by the priest. The breast was to be waved, and eaten by the worshipper. The scriptural notices of these rites are to be found in Ex. 29:24-28; Lev. 7:30-34, 8:27, 9:21, 10:14-15; Num. 6:20, 18:11, 18:26-29. Bishop, God said you don't have to lie to get what you need, because He said in Phil. 4:19 - that He would supply all your needs, and Jesus said ask the Father anything in My name, the Father will give it to you. Bishop, and Pastor, God has scriptures in His Bible to go to on giving, not by man's misguided ideas. In Heb. 4:12 - God knows why you are asking for tithes and heave offerings.

Here is what Abram gave Melchizedek

Gen. 14:10 "Now the valley of Siddim was full of tar pits; and the Kings of Sodom and Gomorrah fled, and they fell into them. But those who survived fled to the hill."

Gen. 14:11 "Then they took all the goods of Sodom and Gomorrah and all their food supply, and departed."

Gen. 14:12 "And they also took Lot, Abram's nephew, and his possessions and departed, for he was living in Sodom."

Gen. 14:13 "Then a fugitive came and told Abram the Hebrew. Now he was living by the oaks of Mamre the Amorite, brother of Eschol and brother of Aner, and these were allies with Abram."

Gen. 14:14 "And when Abram heard that his relative had been taken captive, he led out his trained me, born in his house, three hundred and eighteen, and went in pursuit as far as Dan."

Gen. 14:15 "And he divided his servants, and defeated them, and pursued them as far as Hobah, which is north of Damascus."

Gen. 14:16 "And he brought back all the goods, and also brought back his relative Lot with his possessions, and also the women, and the people."

Bishop, and Pastor - God's word is infallible, without error or mistaken. When you read Gen. 14:16 - the truth will come to light about what Abram gave Melchizedek as tithes. Gen. 14:20 says he gave him a tenth of all. Gen. 14:16 says all means goods. I know that you, Bishop Clarence McZendon, and Pastor thought this truth would never come to light. Remember, God's word is the light of this world and cannot be hidden in darkness.

1 Sam. 30:8 "And David inquired of the Lord, saying, Shall I pursue this band? Shall I overtake them? And He said to him, Pursue, for you shall surely overtake them, and you shall surely rescue all."

Cross Ref. 1 Sam 30:8, Ex. 15:9 "The enemy said, I will pursue, I will overtake, I will divided the spoil."

1 Sam. 30:16 "And when he had brought him down, behold, they were spread over all the land, eating and drinking and dancing because of all the great spoil that they had taken from the land of the Philistines and from the land of Judah."

1 Sam. 30:17 "And David slaughtered them from the twilight until the evening of the next day; and not a man of them escaped, except four hundred young men who rode on camels and fled."

1 Sam. 30:18 "So David recovered all that the Amalekites had taken, and rescued his two wives." Cross ref. Gen. 14:16.

1 Sam. 30:19 "But nothing of theirs was missing, whether small or great, sons or daughters, spoil or anything that they had taken for themselves; David brought it all back."

King James Version Living Bible says in Gen. 14:16 "And recovered everything that had been taken, his relative Lot, and all of Lot's possessions, including the women and other captives." Cross ref. 1 Sam. 30:8, 18,19.

These were things Abram took in war in Gen. 14:15-16 and brought back all goods and all spoil in Heb. 7:4. "Now observe how great this man was to whom Abraham, the patriarch, gave a tenth of choicest spoil." Not money, but spoil.

Gen. 14:17 "And the King of Sodom went out to meet him after his return from the slaughter of Chedorlaomer, and the Kings that were with him, at the valley of Shaveh, which is the King's dale."

Gen. 14:18 "And Melchizedek King of Salem brought out bread and wine; now he was a priest of God Most High."

Gen. 14:19 "And blessed him, and said Blessed be Abram of the most God, possessor of heaven and earth."

Gen. 14:20 - King James Version Living Bible says "Then Abram gave Melchizedk a tenth of all the loot."

1 Sam. 30:16 "And when he had brought him down, behold, they were spread over all the land, eating and drinking and dancing because of all the great spoil that they had taken from the land of the Philistines and from the land of Judah. The great spoil was sheep and cattle and other livestock. It says in 1 Sam. 30:20, This is what God's Holy inspired infallible word says, this was spoil that Abram gave Melchizedek as a tenth of tithes. In Heb. 7:4 - Living Bible - Gen. 14:20 - But our Bishops and Pastors are saying this was money he gave him. Bishop and Pastor, read this scripture - Rev. 22:18-19.

1 Sam. 30:22 "Then all the wicked and worthless men among those who went with David answered and said, Because they did not go with us, we will not give them any of the spoil. It was sheep and cattle and livestock that Abram gave Melchizedek as a tent of tithes, as it says in Heb. 7:4.

1 Sam. 30:25 "And so it has been from that day forward, that He made it a statutes and ordinances for Israel to this day."

Gen. 14:21 "And the King of Sodom said to Abram, Give the people to me and take the goods for yourself."

Gen. 14:22 "And Abram said to the King of Sodom, I have sworn to the Lord God Most High, Possessor of heaven and earth."

Gen. 14:23 "That I will not take a thread or a sandal thong or anything that is yours, lest you should say, I have made Abram rich."

Gen. 14:24 "I will take nothing except what the young men have eaten, and the share of the men who went with me, Aner, Eshcol and Mamre; let them take their share."

✳ Chapter 13

Things said by some Pastors or Bishops to deceive us.

Pastor Marilyn Hickey, Pastor Walt Mills, Dr. Frederick Price, Pastor Benny Hinn, Pastor John Hagee, Pastor Creflo Dollar, Pastor Jesse Duplantis, Pastor Mac Hammond, Pastor Chris LeGrande, Pastor R.W. Schambach, Pastor Rod Parsley, Pastor Kenneth Copeland, Bishop Blake, Bishop Gilbert E. Patterson.

Pastor Marilyn Hickey - you said on Channel 40 that Jesus receives our tithes; that's wrong and false. Tithes are not money. Why are you teaching tithes, when God said in Rom. 1:18 "For the wrath of God is revealed from heaven against all unrighteousness, and ungodliness of men, who suppress the truth in unrighteousness."

Pastor Walt Mills, and Pastor John Hagee, Pastor Jesse Duplantis, Pastor Mac Hammond - How can you as Pastors teach tithing in God's Church today? You are teaching on Channel 40 saying we should tithe. This is wicked, and morally wrong. Don't you know that Christ is the end of the law? (Rom. 10:4) Heb. 8:13 (Read Eph. 2:1-5)

Pastor John Hagee on Channel 40 - you said Jesus was teaching tithes in Matt. 23. That's wrong, when you read that scripture it says they tithe mint and dill, and cummin. This is what God said about tithes in Deu. 14:22 "to tithe all the produce from what you sow, which comes out of the field every year, mint and dill, and cummin came out of the field. This was what Jesus said tithes were - not money. He believed they placed too much emphasis on minor details, while ignoring "the weightier provisions of the law", such as "justice and mercy and faithfulness."

Pastor Benny Hinn, How is giving going to stop evil, and why would you say, if we made a pledge to God, like giving $20,000 and you don't keep your promise, God will not bless you. No scripture supports you in this lie. God says in Matt. 15:19 "Out of your heart proceed evil thoughts." Don't you know, Pastor, God has put scripture in His Holy Bible about false teachers like you and all Pastors that are teaching tithes are false teachers because tithes are not money. In 2 Tim. 3:16 "God says all scripture is given by inspiration of God, and is profitable for doctrine, for reproof, for correction, for instruction in righteousness." Lying about anything is not obeying that scripture. 2 Tim 3:16 and Heb. 4:12 There is coming a day, Pastor, when God is going to judge you all on the secrets of your heart on tithes being money.

Pastor Rod Parsley, Why are you teaching the tree in the Garden of Eden represents tithes?

Pastor Chris LeGrande - God is no repecter of persons; why then do you say the tither stands up first, and bring your tithes? God says in 1 Pet. 5:3 "Neither being lords over God's heritage, but being examples to the flock."

Dr. Frederick Price "All the teaching you do each week, don't you know that tithes are not money. You know this, why do you ask people to send their tithes to you? This is morally wrong. Why don't you use a scripture like I have in this book to show your members that there are scriptures that say what tithes are. Why don't you teach against tithes, knowing all Pastors that are teaching tithes are teaching false and misleading doctrine? Pastor Creflo Dollar - you were teaching falsely by teaching that tithes are for us today. You also said on Channel 40 that you should build a machine in your church and everyone that puts his card in it, if it says no tither, then you should line them up and shoot them. Tithes are not for us, and are not money. How can you be so deceptive?

Pastor Kenny Copeland - Why agree with your friend Creflo Dollar, knowing all the time he was teaching wrong, and falsely about tithes being money and being for us today. This is evil, wicked and deceptive. Pastor, this is unrighteousness, and ungodly on your part, when He said in 1 Pet. 5:2 - Don't preach His word for filthy lucre. Pastor Kenny Copeland, you are agreeing with Pastors that are teaching false doctrine about tithes.

Pastor, you are all teaching false doctrine on tithes for sordid gain. 2 Tim. 3:16 - The whole Bible was given to us by inspiration from God and is useful to teach us what is true and make us realize what is wrong in our lives. It straightens us out and helps us do what is right.

2 Tim. 4:3 "For the time will come when they will not endure sound doctrine; but wanting to have their ears tickled, they will accumulate for themselves teachers in accordance to their own desires.

Pastors that are taking tithes should believe God's word by faith, not on your misguide ideas.

R.W. Schambach, you also said on Channel 40, if we don't pay our tithes, we are sinning. There is not a scripture to support your lie, and tithes are not money. This is sinful, and wicked. You also said we should pay our tithes up front when it says in Deu. 14:22 to tithe once a year, and in Deu. 26:12 every third year. How can you pay tithes when tithes are not money? Pastor R.W. Schambach, you said also that God spoke to you to ask you to tell thousands and thousands of people to pledge $2000 and God said that He would bless them in 90 days. Well, you lied again. How can you be so deceitful?

Here are scriptures to show that God doesn't speak to us any more, like He did long ago.

Heb. 1:1 - New Open Bible New American Standard "God, after He spoke long ago to the fathers in the prophets in many portions and in many ways." Cross References John 9:29, 16:13.

Heb. 1:2 "In these last days has spoken to us in His Son, whom He appointed heir of all things, through whom also He made the world." Cross References Matt. 13:39

Heb. 1:1 King James Version and the Living Bible "God, who at sundry times and divers manners spake in time past unto the fathers by the prophets.

Heb. 1:1 - Living Bible - Long ago God spoke in many different ways to our fathers through the prophets in visions, dreams, and even face to face, telling them little by little about His plans."

Heb. 1:2 "Hath in these last days spoken unto us by His Son, whom He hath appointed heir of all things, by whom also He made the world."

Heb. 1:2 - Living Bible - "But now in these days He has spoken to us through His Son by whom He made the world and everything therein.

Pastor R. W. Schambach, you said on TV, that God spoke to you. Why didn't He say to you stop lying about tithes being money, and that money doesn't finance Christ's coming back? Pastor R.W. Schambach, it is impossible to separate God from His word, because the Word of God, and the Spirit of God agree in all things concerning His Word. If He spoke to you then He would be contradicting Himself, because in His Word, the Bible, He said how to give, but you are saying He spoke and said to you to ask us to give $2000 and He said He no longer speaks to us in Heb. 1:1-2. You are saying this on TV that God spoke to you. You are lying. God does not speak to us anymore. Read Heb. 1:1-2, Pastor. You are saying things to impress people into believing that God is speaking to you. If He did, He wouldn't be a true God.

There is coming a day, Pastor R.W. Schambach, when God is going to judge us all on the secrets of our hearts. One may be useful in this world in serving God's plans and yet fail to qualify for eternal life in that day when God shall judge the secrets of men's hearts.

Pastor Paul Crouch, you are president of TBN. How can you as a pastor and man of God allow anyone to come on your TV station and teach tithing and agree with them?

2 John 10:11 "Don't be a partaker of their evil deeds," and in 1 John 5:17 - "All unrighteousness is sin." But you, Pastor Paul Crouch, why would you say things to deceive God's flock by your scandalous teaching about building an altar as you did on TV? Then you and your group did offer up people's debts on this altar to God. This is unrighteous, for you and your group knowing this is false to teach something like this. Don't you, Pastor, have any respect for Christians that are coming to God that are new-born Christians? They don't know their Bible, but have their trust in a Pastor believing he won't mislead them falsely. They are accepting what you are saying about an altar as true. This is very deceitful on your part. Pastor Paul Crouch, this is idol worship. When God said in John 17:17 "To sanctify them in the truth; they word is true." He didn't mean building an altar to God. Have we all, Pastor Paul Crouch, become a Nation of idol worshippers by building an altar to offer up debts to God. The only thing we offer up to God (Heb. 13:15). Through Him then, let us continually offer up a sacrifice of praise to God, that is the fruit of our lips that give thanks to His

name." And in Rom. 12:1 "I beseech you therefore, brethren, by the mercies of God, that ye present your bodies a living sacrifice, holy, acceptable unto God, which is your reasonable service." No Pastor or person can offer up anything on an altar, only if you are a Levi priest. God said to Moses in Ex. 27, How to make an altar. The one you have used every year is false. Only God can tell you what to build. Ex. 27 - Only a Levite priest can offer up the five offerings.

God is saying in Psalms 14:3 - Pastor, "that all have strayed away, all are rotten with sin."

God is saying to us all Pastors have strayed away from His word, to teach fables on tithes and building an altar for us today.

Chapter 14

Principles in giving, now that the Law is over, for the nation of Israel.

2 Cor. 9:6-9 (6) "Now this I say, he who sows sparingly shall also reap sparingly; and he who sows bountifully shall also reap bountifully."

6. But remember this - if you give little, you will get little. A farmer who plants just a few seeds will get only a small crop, but if he plants much he will reap much." King James Version and The Living Bible.

7.. "Every man according as he purposeth in his heart, so let him give; not grudgingly, or of necessity; for God loveth a cheerful giver."
Every one must make up his own mind as to how much should give; Don't force anyone to give more than he really wants to, for cheerful givers are the ones God prizes.

Principles in giving: 2 Cor. 9:6-8 There is no better indi -cator of growth in the new life than in the area of giv- " ing. This passage deals with the attitude one should have in his giving - it should be cheerful. When giving is cheerful, it will also be generous. The important rule of thumb is not how much is given but how much is left after the giving. God is not primarily occupied with the amount of the gift, but with the motive that lies behind it. All the money in the world belongs to God. My gift to Him does not make Him richer, it makes me spiritually richer because of the realization that everything I have is His and that I am giving because I love Him and want to give.

The formula for giving is found in 1 Corinthians 16:2 - where three principles can be seen: (1) My giving is to be regular, "On the first day of every week" (2) My giving is to be systematic, "Let each one of you put aside and save," and (3) My giving is to be proportionate, as he may prosper."

1 Cor. 16:2 "Upon the first day of the week let every one of you lay by him in store, as God hath prospered him, that there be no gatherings when I come, put aside and save, as he may prosper."

What About The Storehouse

No doubt many of you have heard it said at some time or other, that the local church is the storehouse. They fail to see that this command was given to the Jew under the law. Since there is no law or commandments to tithe today.

We Are Not Under the Law, But Grace

Now in view of these facts, there is no storehouse in this dispensation. Here is the plain simple truth about giving to the Lord's works. In Old Testament times our Lord expressed His will by tithing law. Disobedience brought punishment. Under grace our Lord expresses his will, not by law, but in plain simple statements.

God's Word forbids us to mix law and grace, Col. 2:16 and Gal. 5:1 - Under law, men paid tithes because of fear. Failure to tithe under law brought wrath. Failure to give liberally under grace brings no rewards. Under grace men give because they love the Lord Jesus and His Gospel. Under law, the people gave because they had to. Under grace they give because they want to. That is, the Holy Spirit in men causes them to be willing and eager to give. Rom. 8:4 and Heb. 8:1.

A Bomb on Tithing

There are two or three more scriptures on tithing that I would like to discuss with you. I wish that I could get every storehouse tithing enthusiast to read Deu. 14:22-26. Please read and notice:

Jesus and Tithing

We have only three places recorded where the Lord Jesus ever mentioned tithing - Matt. 23:23. In this scripture, what they tithed were mints and anise and cummin, which God said to them to tithe. It came out of the field every year in Deu. 14:22 - not money. Luke 11:42 - in every instance the Lord Jesus was speaking to the unbelieving Pharisees - those who were under the law. Matt. 23:23 and Luke 11:42 - You will notice in this passage that Christ was speaking to the Pharisees, and He told them that under the law, their obligations were greater than just paying tithes.

Why did Jesus say that the unsaved Pharisees should practice tithing? Because they were under the law, and the law commanded it, not grace.

However, Jesus never said one word about tithing when

speaking to His disciples. Now is it right to take what Jesus said to unbelieving Pharisees (who were under the law) and apply the same to those who are under grace? Isn't this a little illogical?

There is not one scripture where Christ ever enjoined tithing on born again believers. Christ no where taught His disciple to observe tithing. Tithing was for the disciples of Moses, not for the disciple of Christ. (John 1:17)

We must always be careful as we study the word of God to ascertain whether God is speaking to people under Law or Grace. It certainly is wrong to apply that which is written for the Jew under the Law about tithing to apply it to us of the Church of God, and yet that is exactly what most of those who teach til the advocate that the Church is the storehouse for tithing.

The Law which the Christian should be concerned about is the Law of Love, not the Law of Moses. We're under the Law of Love when we're saved and this comprehends all laws which man should keep. (Rom. 13:10, Gal.5:14, John 13:34, Matt. 22:37-39.)

Abraham's tithes "was not brought to any storehouse" or sanctuary. (See Genesis 14:17-24)

New Testament Giving

The subject of giving is clearly brought out in the New Testament and there is no excuse for anyone to resort to the Old Testament and the law to teach how we should give. Now let's look at the New Testament principles of giving. Let us consider some portions of scripture that establish the norms for our financial stewardship in this dispensation of grace.

Christian Giving Should Be Done Secretly

In regard to Christian, "giving" the Lord Jesus admonished that it should be done with discretion or secretly "when thou doest alms, let not thy left hand know what thy right hand doeth." Matt. 6:1-5.

Giving by means of "tithing," is the very opposite of this. You have to count it, speak of it, make it known, and quite a number of people will become aware how much one earns and how much one is giving. The entire system of tithing is linked up with other things which are not in the Spirit of New Testament teaching tithing by the law is opposite of this. God said in this scripture, Matt. 6:1-5 - Don't let your left hand know what your right hand is doing. When you are doing a charitable deed, to be seen by them, otherwise you have no reward from your Father in Heaven. The entire system of tithing is linked up with other thing which are not in the spirit of New Testament teaching.

Christian Giving Is A Personal Matter

1 Cor. 16:2 - This scripture is very plain in telling us that giving is a personal matter and done secretly in this dispensation of grace. A personal matter, under grace. He expresses His will not by law. Notice the phrase, let every one of you. Let every one of you - father, mother, son, and children do his own giving. Each one of us must do own repenting, each one of us must do our own praying. Each one of us must do our own dying, and each one of us must do our own giving.

No preacher nor leader in the church has any right to dictate or tell you how much to give or where you should give. That is strictly between you and the Lord. It is no body's business where or how much you give. The Holy Spirit will lead you in your giving if you will seek His guidance.

Christian Giving Should Be Voluntary

Born again believers should be ready and willing to give at all times - wherever the Holy Spirit shows us there is a need. Going back to 1 Cor. 16:1-2, we have a good example of this kind of giving. The Apostle Paul said, now concerning that collection for the saints. Apostle Paul urged each Corinthian believer to lay aside so much money according "as God hath prospered him."

Let us realize once and for all that there is no church storehouse in this dispensation of grace. Old Testament scripture on the storehouse - Neh. 13:12, 10:35-39. The church is the Body of Christ, not a storehouse.

Christian Giving Must Be Spirit-Directed

In Gal. 5:18, we read, "If ye be led of the Spirit, ye are not under the law." The law was God's ordinances, that tithing was under, which we were not under as Gentiles. Christ in Col. 2:14, nailing the law to the cross. Eph. 2:15. Now we know according to Matt. 23:23, Heb. 7:5 and Lev. 27:30-34 - that tithing was a part of the law. We are under grace. Tithing was part of the Old Covenant that was done away in Christ in Eph. 2:15. Now, some Pastors are putting their people and themselves under the law of tithing, which were God's ordinance did away by Christ. In Eph. 2:15 - abolished in His flesh at the cross, the law of commandments contained in ordinances having wiped out the handwriting of requirements to that was against us which was contrary to us. And Christ took it all away, having nailed it to the Cross.

In this dispensation of grace, all of our giving must be Spirit-directed. Read this scripture from the Amplified Bible - New Testament. "But now, we are discharged from the Law and have terminated all intercourse with it. Having died to what once restrained us and held us captive. So now, we serve not under (obedience to) the old code of written regulations, but (under obedience) to the promptings of the Spirit in newness (of life.) Rom. 7:6

Beloved, the law is not our standard of living today. Today, it is no longer what the law requires. But what the Spirit would have us to do. To practice tithing today, when tithing is not money, is to go back to the ordinances of God's law which is over. It is exact opposite of serving God in newness and of the Spirit.

There is nothing in the Bible which tells the sons of God how much they are to give. That was left up to only the Nations of Israel. In Heb. 7:5 and in Num. 18:26, that was left up to each believer and "the leadership of the Spirit." 2 Cor. 9:7 "Let every one give as he has made up his mind and purposed in his heart, not reluctantly or sorrowfully or under compulsion."

By all means, give to the Lord's cause. Give all you can. But in your giving, ignore the law on tithing — all of its terms, decrees and demands. They were nailed to the cross and completely wiped away by the death of Christ. (Eph. 2:15, Col. 2:1 and 3:4)

Let us no longer listen to the law or commandment or ordinance on tithing or its decrees. Christ forever made us free from all that from the law of fleshly commandment (Read Heb. 8:13 and Rom. 4:10.) But let us yield ourselves in humble submission to the Spirit of God not the ordinances of the Law. He will lead us in all our giving, and in every thought and deed. There is no other way to have victory over the flesh with all its pride, greed, love for pleasure, desire to satisfy self and all other longings. It is the only way to conquer all fleshly desires and habits. Victory can never come through by listening to the law on tithing. Its demand is gone for us as Gentiles. It can only come through absolute surrender to the Spirit of God on giving to let Him lead us in all our service, deeds, thoughts and actions. "Walk in the Spirit, and ye shall not fulfill the lust of the flesh." (Gal. 5:16).

We need more Spirit-led giving and less preacher-led giving. Spirit-led giving always honors God and promotes scriptural things. Let the Spirit lead you in your giving and you will never go wrong.

Christian Giving Must Be Done Willingly

We are not to give to ease our conscience. We are not to give because we feel that we have to give. We are not to give to make a name for ourselves. We are not to give because others give. Rather, the born-again believer gives because he loves the Lord and because of what Christ has done for him.

Read this enlightening scripture: "For if there be first a willing mind, it is accepted according tot hat a man hath, and not according to that he hath not." (2 Cor. 8:12) Here is the supreme difference between giving under the law and grace.

Grace is undeserved, unmerited favor bestowed on sinful man because God so loved that He gave. Similarly, the only gift that God accepts in this age of grace is that which comes from a heart constrained by this same love. Any gift tarnished or cheapened by any other motive is unacceptable. God asks and wants no more than we will give willingly.

Christian Giving Should Be Done Cheerfully

If we have right motives in giving, god is going to bless . us. What is the right motive? Read the Word of God.

We can settle this whole question of money if we would realize once and for all that all of your money really belongs to

God. When we are saved, every thing we have, including our body, time, and money, belongs to Him who loved us and redeemed us with His own precious blood. That's why God's Word says, "Ye are not your own for ye are brought with a price." (1 Cor. 6:19 - 20) God says, "The silver is mine, and the gold is mine, saith the Lord of Hosts." (Hag. 2:8)

Liberal Giving is God's Plan

When we compare the Old Testament teachings on giving with those in the New Testament, we find there is a vast difference. Under the Old Testament law, people were forced to give. Under grace, a Christian gives because he loves to give.

Many times the question comes up, "How much should a believer give to the Lord?" Well, maybe you can give $5.00 a week or maybe it's just 50 cents. But whatever the amount, God says "if there be first a willing min, it is accepted according to that a man hath, and not according to that he hath not." (2 Cor. 8:12) God not only considers what we give, but what we keep as well, and we are responsible to Him for it all. He tell us too, that "he which soweth sparingly, shall reap sparingly; and he which soweth bountifully, shall reap also bountifully." (2 Cor. 9:6)

Christian giving should not be done for the sake of reward, but God promised a reward to those who give liberally out of a heart of love. One who really loves the Savior and His work, usually gives with a cheerful heart. It is as natural as the sun shining for that person to give.

A Bomb On Tithing

I am sure that you can see the mischief that results when one tries to mix the Covenant of Law with the Liberty of Grace. This scripture - Deu. 14:22-26 says that the Jew could spend his tithes for wine or for strong drink. The "storehouse tithing enthusiast," will find himself in bad shape if he tries to live by this scripture. These verses plainly tell us that the Jews could spend their tithes on beer and whiskey. Any one should be able to see that these instructions were given to the Nation of Israel long before the full revelation of Christian living was given to the Church through the Apostle Paul. How necessary it is that God's people lean to rightly divide the Word of Truth on tithing were and who were to pay tithes. (2 Tim. 2:15)

The Living Bible 1 Cor. 16:2 - On every Lord's day each of you should put aside something from what you have earned during the week, and use it for this offering. The amounts depend on how much the Lord has helped you earn. Don't wait until I get there and then try to collect it all at once.

Luke 6:38 "And it will be given to you, good measure, pressed down, shaken together, running over, they will pour into your lap. For by your standard of measured to you in return."

Acts 20:35 "In everything I showed you that by working hard in this manner you must help the weak, and remember the words of the Lord Jesus that He Himself said, It is more blessed to give than to receive."

God put these scriptures in His Holy Bible so that there will not be any confusion.

"If there come any unto you believing not this doctrine, receive him not into your house, neither bid him God speed; for he that biddeth him God speed is partaking of his evil deeds." (2 John 10:11)

Tithes are the doctrine of God. If your church is not giving you spiritual food, or holding to the doctrine of Christ, God says that you should not be a partaker of their evil deeds by giving them His money.

In closing, let me say that there is no rule governing the giving of a Christian except that he is to give freely, liberally, and cheerfully. So, my dear friends, if you are born-again, the God who called you and who saved you, will guide you as to where, when, and how much to give. If you will not lose your reward, all that God expects from us is a willing heart. As Christians, let us bear in mind the statement of our blessed Lord. "It is more blessed to give than to receive." (Acts 20:35)

Christian Giving Must Be Done Willingly

WHAT TITHING IS NOT – WHAT NATION IS HE SPEAKING TO

Chapter 15

Temptation by Satan

God said that the greatest sin is self-will. Pastor, you have left the word and will of God for you as a Pastor, and have turned to your own will. It seems like Satan has taken the word of God from your heart and has blinded your eyes. "Why do you call Me, Lord, Lord, and don't keep or do My Father's will."

Of all the possible sins against God, Pastor, the most serious is that of self-will. This sin led to the fall of Satan (Isa. 14:12-14) and it can be said to be the root of Adam's transgression. (Gen. 3:1-7) It is therefore of most importance that the child of god find his will and perform it. The Holy Spirit will convince the willing heart of its power. "All scripture is inspired of God," wrote the Christian Apostle Paul - " and is profitable for teaching, for reproof, for correction, for training in righteousness." (2 Tim. 3:16)

It seems that some Pastor's will is to change God's word, which is immutable, about tithes being money.

This was Satan's will to be like God. You, Pastor, are saying I will be like God and change His immutable word about tithes, and saying in your heart my thoughts are above His. I will make myself like the Most High, by changing His Word. You are saying in your heart, I will ascend my thoughts above the clouds, and be like God as I have changed His word, to my glory. Satan has blinded your eyes, Pastor, about tithes.

Pastor, the role of Satan against Christians is to blind their eyes and to make confusion in their minds about God's word. He can appear as a hideous dragon. It is well summed up by the meaning of the name Satan - Adversary. He is also called "the devil," meaning "accuser." He can appear as a hideous dragon or as a beautifully deceptive "angel of light." He stands hatefully opposed to all the work of God and the truth of God's word, and resourcefully promotes defiance among men. (2 Cor. 11:14, Rev. 12:9, Mark 4:15, Job 2:4-5.)

When Satan sinned, he was expelled from heaven - Luke 10:18 "And He said to them, I was watching Satan fall from heaven like lightning"; although apparently he still had some access to God. (Job 1:6) A multitude of angels cast in their lot with him in his fall and subsequently became the demons mentioned often in the Bible. Matt. 12:24 "But when the Pharisees heard it, they said, This man casts out demons only by Beelzebul the ruler of the demons." Satan's doom was secured by Jesus' death on the cross (John 16:11) Because the ruler of this world has been judged, he will continue to hinder God's word and program and blind your minds and hearts about tithes, until he and his angels are cast into the lake of fire. Matt. 25:41 "Then He will also say to those on His left, Depart from Me, accursed ones, into the eternal fire which has been prepared for the devil and his angels."

Rev. 20:10 - This is what God is saying to all you false teachers that are supering His word falsely by lying about tithes. "And the devil who deceived them [like you, Pastor] has deceived My flock about tithes, for the love of money, then was cast into the lake of fire and brimstone, where the beast and the false prophet are, and they will be tormented day and night for ever and ever."

Living Bible Rev. 20:10 "Then the devil who had betrayed them will again be thrown into the Lake of Fire burning with sulphur where the Creature and False Prophet are, and they will be tormented day and night forever and ever."

The terrifying work of Satan, the unbeliever, is described in Scripture as follows: "he blinds their minds." 2 Cor. 4:4 - In this case, the god of this world has blinded the minds of the unbelieving, that they might not see the light of the gospel of the glory of Christ, who is the image of God. He takes the Word of God from their hearts." Luke 8:12 "And those beside the road are those who have heard; then the devil comes and takes away the word from their heart"; so that they may not believe and be saved, and he controls the. Acts 13:8 "But Elymas the magician [for thus his name is translated] was opposing them, seeking to turn the proconsul away from the faith." In regard to Christians, Satan may accuse them, Rev. 12:10 "Then, I heard a loud voice shouting across the heavens. It has happened at last; God's salvation and power and the rule, and the authority of his Christ are finally here, for the Accuser of our brothers has been thrown down from heaven on to earth - he accused them day and night before our God, devouring their testimony." 1 Pet. 5:8 "Be of sober spirit, be on the alert. Your adversary, the devil, prowls about like a roaring lion, seeking someone to devour, deceive them." 2 Cor. 11:14 "And no wonder, for even Satan disguises himself as an angel of light, hinder their work." 2 Cor. 11:15 "Therefore it is not surprising if his servants also disguise themselves as servants of righteousness; whose end shall be according to their deeds, hinder their work of unrighteousness." 1 Thess. 2:18 "For we wanted to come to you, I Paul, more than once - and yet Satan thwarted us." 1 Cor. 7:5 "Stop depriving one another, except by agreement for a time that you may devote yourselves to prayer, and come together again lest Satan tempt you because of your lack of self-control;" Satan has even been used by God to discipline Christians, 1 Cor. 5:5 "I have decided to deliver such a one to Satan for destruction of his flesh, that his spirit may be saved in the day of the Lord Jesus." 2Cor. 12:7 "And because of the surpassing greatness of the revelations for this reason, to keep me from exalting myself, there was given me a thorn in the flesh, a messenger of Satan to buffet me - to keep me from exalting myself."

The Christian's response to Satan is to recognize his power and deception, 2 Cor. 2:11 "In order that no advantage be taken of us by Satan; for we are not ignorant of his schemes." Matt. 4:10 "Then Jesus said to him, Begone, Satan: For it is written, You shall worship the Lord your God, and serve Him only, fulfill religious duty to Him only." Eph. 6:11 "Put on the full armor of God, that you may be able to stand firm against the scheme of the devil, to adhere steadfastly to the faith." 1 Pet. 5:9 "But resist him, firm in your faith, knowing that the same experiences of your suffering are being accomplished by your brethren who are in the world." Jam. 4:7 "Submit therefore to God. Resist the devil and he will flee from you, and do not give him opportunities."

Jam. 4:8 "Draw near to God and He will draw near to you. Cleanse your hands you sinner; and purify your hearts, you doubleminded." Isa. 1:16 "Wash yourselves, make yourselves clean; Remove the veil of your deeds from My sight; cease to do evil." 1 Pet. 5:6 "Humble yourselves, therefore, under the mighty hand of God, that He may exalt you at the proper time. And not to give him [Devil] an opportunity." Eph. 4:27 - In practice, the best way to oppose him is to be a growing Christian. Also, in the light of the devil's tremendous power to blind men to the gospel. Christians must always be aggressively and compassionately witnessing in order to snatch themselves from Satan's control. Acts 26:18 "To open their eyes so that they may turn from darkness to light and from the dominion of Satan to

God; in order that they may receive forgiveness of sins, and an inheritance among those who have been sanctified by faith in Christ." Believers can respond to temptation by Satan with confidence. But, we know that nothing can separate us from the love of God. Rom. 8:28.

1 Peter 3:17 "For it is better, if God will it so, that you suffer for doing what is right rather than for what is wrong."

Chapter 16

For Pastors That Are Receiving Tithes

This message is for all Pastors, knowing God's Word but not honoring His word, who have turned to their own righteousness about tithes, and knowing that tithes were not money, and that tithing was for the nation of Israel only. Pastor, I am sorry to say this, there is no scripture in the Bible that says tithes were money or that tithes were paid each week. How can you, Pastor, teach something that is not in the holy scripture? It is for sordid gain, love of money. Prov. 15:27 says "He who profits illicitly troubles his own house." The money you take is not permitted, sanctioned, or allowed by law, or by tradition.

God is saying in 1 Pet. 5:2 - To all you Pastors, to feed the flock of God which is among you, taking the oversight thereof, not by constraint, but willingly, not for filthy lucre, but of a ready mind. John 21:15-17 "So when they had finished breakfast, Jesus said to Simon Peter, Simon, son of Jonas, do you love Me more than these? He said to Him, yes, Lord; you know that I love you; He said to him, tend to My lambs." (16) "He saith to him again the second time, Simon, son of Jonas, lovest thou Me? He saith unto him, Yes, Lord, thou knowest that I love thee. He saith unto him, Feed My sheep." (17) "He saith unto him the third time, Simon, son of Jonas, lovest thou Me? Peter was grieved because He said unto him, Lord, thou knowest all things, thou knowest that I love thee. Jesus said unto him, Feed My sheep."

God is saying to all Pastors today the same thing He said to the nation of Israel. "Return to My word." 1 Pet. 5:2 - He says not to preach His Word for sordid gain, and also to feed and shepherd His flock. God said to Simon if you love Me feed My sheep. Feeding His sheep on the Word of God's infallible inspiration, Pastor, not for what you can get out of it. But God says in Rom. 1:18 "For the wrath of God is revealed from heaven against all ungodliness and unrighteousness of men, who suppress the truth in unrighteousness."

Instruction for the true Teacher

1 Tim. 4:7 "But have nothing to do with Worldly fable fit only for old women. On the other hand, discipline yourself for the purpose of godliness."

Last Message For Pastors and Prophets
Teaching Tithes Falsely

God is saying in His scripture, anyone that is putting tithing in His Church is not a true Pastor or Prophet. A Pastor or Prophet that is asking for tithes, are both false. Jesus said that you will know them by their fruits. You will know the tree by its fruit. Beware of false prophets, and false teachers. Matt. 7:15 - Cross Ref. to Matt. 24:11-24, Matt: 7:16-20 - Cross Ref. to Matt: 12:33, Luk. 6:44, Matt. 7:21 - Cross Ref. to Luke 6:46 - Cross Ref. to Mal. 1:6 "A son honors his father, and a servant, his master. Then if I am a father, where is My honor? And if I am a master, where is My respect? says the Lord of Hosts to you, Oh priests who despise My name. But you say How have we despised Thy name?" My saying to you, Pastor, and Prophets, you have despised God's name by not honoring or respecting His word on tithes. Matt. 7:15-27, Matt: 7:23 - Cross Ref. to Psa. 6:8 "Depart from Me, all you who do iniquity." Psa. 119:115 "Depart from Me, evildoers that I may observe the commandments of My god." Cross Ref. to Luk. 13:27 "And he will say, I tell you, I do not know where you are from; Depart from Me, all you evildoers." Matt. 25:41 "Then he will also say to those on His left, Depart from Me, accursed ones, into the eternal fire which has been prepared for the devil and his angels."

You, Pastor, and false Prophets, are asking for tithes knowing this is wrong and a lie. Matt. 15:19 "For out of the heart come evil thoughts, murders, adulteries, fornications, thefts, false witness, lying and slanders. As God said in Psa. 116:11 "I said in My haste; all men are liars, but all My scripture are given for instruction in righteousness. Pastor and Prophets who are lying about tithes, 1 Cor. 10:21 - that are taking tithes in My Church. 1 Cor. 10:21 "You cannot drink the cup of the Lord and the cup of demons. You cannot partake of the table of the Lord and the table of demons. Ye cannot drink from the cup at the Lord's table and at Satan's table, too you cannot eat bread both at the Lord's table and at Satan's table."

Pastor, you can only lie about God's Word about tithes for so long, then He will bring His Word to light. His Word is Him speaking to us, not us speaking to Him. (Rom. 2:16) "The day will surely come when at God's command Jesus Christ will judge the secret lives of everyone, their inmost thoughts and motive."

Remember, some of you Pastors will say it doesn't make any difference how we should give, by tithing or any way. Sorry, but God's Holy Bible is His Word. He is speaking to us. He said that He has put scripture in His Bible on how we are to give, NOT ON MAN'S OPINIONS OR HIS MISGUIDED IDEAS. But on His Word. 2Tim 3:16 - it says all scripture is inspired by God.

God is asking you, Pastor, do you love Me, as He asked Peter. You say yes, but why do some of you practice tithing in My church, which is wrong and immoral by lying about Me, when you say I said for you to take tithes?

Don't you think, it is about time to free My flock from under this CURSE that tithes were under Christ; He nailed the Law to the Cross that tithes were under. They have never been money.

Pastors who know that it is wrong for any Pastor to ask for tithes have been in Church and not said anything to God's flock. How can you call yourself His shepherds? A good shepherd watches over his flock, God's Flock. "For false teachers come in sheep's clothing, but inwardly are like ravenous wolves, and see wrong and turn your back on it." Like tithing. A good shepherd always lay down his life for his flock.

May God's blessing be upon you. I hope this Book shed
some light about tithes.
God bless you, my sisters and Brothers in
Jesus Christ's Name.

(Final – Conclusion)

Scripture shows before Christ's death on the Cross the Levi High Priests didn't own any property as land, but they received *Tithes* as their inheritance *under the Law* (Numbers 18:26). However, in Acts 4: 36-37 it shows that they no longer received *Tithes* as an inheritance. After Christ's death they owned land in Acts 4:36-37, because the *Law* was fulfilled in Christ. *Tithes*, under the *Law*, were over when Christ became the *High Priest*. He was not a Levite. He was of the Tribe of Judah about which Moses said nothing concerning Priests. God didn't call the Tribe of Judah to receive *Tithes*, only to the Tribe of Levi in Heb. 7:5 do these *Laws* and principles apply throughout Eternity. Jews and Gentiles alike are now under *Grace*. Romans 10:4 says Christ is the end of the *Law* that *Tithes* were under. Eph. 2:15 says Christ abolished, in His flesh, the *Enmity* that is of the *Law*. Hebrews 8:13 says now the *Law* is become obsolete ready to vanish away. We are no longer under the *Law*; we are now under *Grace*.

READ: Matt. 15:9 – As in vain doctrine of *Men* teaching worthless doctrine on *Tithes* based on man-made *Laws* instead of those true words of God.

Romans 10:3 – Some pastors are teaching *Tithes*. This is unrighteousness being IGNORANT, seeking to establish their own righteousness about *Tithes*. They have not submitted themselves unto the *truth* about God's word about *Tithes not being money.*

May God's blessings be upon you. I hope
this book sheds some light about what
TITHES and OFFERING
(Malachi 3:8-12)
God bless you, my sisters
and brothers in
Jesus Christ's
name.

213

BOOK AVAILABLE THROUGH

What Tithing Is Not $15.00

Los Angeles, California 90061
(310) 631-4674

Name _____ Date _____
Address _____
City_____ State _____ Zip Code_____
Day telephone _____
Evening telephone_____
Book title _____

Number of books ordered ___ Total cost .... $ _____
Sales Taxes (CA Add 8.25%) .... $ _____
Shipping & Handling $3.55 per book .... $ _____
Total Amount Due.. $ _____
_ Check _ Money Order

_____   _____
Signature   Date

DEUTERONOMY 14:1-29 Unclean and clean Foods

Deut. 14:22 — Be sure to Israelites to set aside a tenth of all your fields produce each year. Eat the tithe of your produce grain, New wine oil, herds flocks etc. in the presence of the Lord your God at the place he will choose as a dwelling for His Name. So you will learn to revere the Lord your God always. But if that place is too distant and you have been blessed by the Lord your God and cannot carry your tithe, because the place where the Lord will choose to put His Name is so far away, then exchange your tithe for silver, and take the silver with you and go to the silver with you and go to the place the Lord your God will choose. (26) USE the silver to buy whatever you Like ——— then you and your household shall eat there in the presence of the Lord your God and rejoice. Don't Neglect the Levite Living in your towns they have No allotment or inheritance of their own. At the end of every three years, bring all the tithes of what that year produce and store it in your town so that the Levites, fatherless widow can eat.

At the end of every seven years you must cancel debts. This is how it is done: Every creditor shall cancel the loan he has made to his fellow Israelite. He shall not require payment from his fellow Israelite brother. Because the Lord's time for cancelling debts has been proclaimed. Cancel any debt your brother owes you

Deuteronomy 16: 16-17 ___ God does Not
Expect us to give more than we can, but
we will be blessed when we give cheerfully
For Some 10 pecent may be a burden, FOR
most of us, that would be far too little
Look at what you have and then give in
proportion to what you have been given

LaVergne, TN USA
01 December 2010

206985LV00003B/116/A